DATE DUE

DEMCO 38-297

By Olga Maynard

The Ballet Companion
The American Ballet
Bird of Fire: The Story of Maria Tallchief

AMERICAN
MODERN DANCERS
The Pioneers

AMERICAN MODERN DANCERS
The Pioneers

by OLGA MAYNARD

An introduction to Modern Dance through the
biographical studies of the first creative dancers of that
art. Related in narrative form, it is also arranged for
teacher-student use in dance classes, complete with
Notes. Illustrated with eight photographs of the dancers.

An Atlantic Monthly Press Book
LITTLE, BROWN and COMPANY
Boston   Toronto

COPYRIGHT © 1965 BY OLGA MAYNARD

LIBRARY OF CONGRESS CATALOG CARD NO. 64-21493

00874 31 RI

SIXTH PRINTING

ATLANTIC—LITTLE, BROWN BOOKS
ARE PUBLISHED BY
LITTLE, BROWN AND COMPANY
IN ASSOCIATION WITH
THE ATLANTIC MONTHLY PRESS

Published simultaneously in Canada
by Little, Brown & Company (Canada) Limited

PRINTED IN THE UNITED STATES OF AMERICA

For
M. FRANCES DOUGHERTY, *Professor*
Department of Physical Education
University of Oregon
and
GENEVIEVE OSWALD, *Curator*
Dance Collection, New York Public Library
and their compeers

Author's Note

THE DANCE style called "Modern" is especially significant to Americans because it is ours. In the twentieth century we inaugurated a form of dance which moved theatre dancing from the stage into the everyday actions, thoughts and feelings of ordinary people. It was timely and new, a contemporary dance, and so it was called "Modern."

The pioneers of this form of dance are the subjects of this book, whose purpose is to relate, in chronological order, their biographies or histories. These inform us about a way of dancing and also about the times in which the dancers lived and worked. I have written this book not only as a record about dancing but with a strong awareness of American history. That history is made not only by scientists and politicians but also by creative artists. American dance, in our century, ranks high among our national art treasures. When an American dancer appears before a foreign audience he serves as ambassador for our culture and society.

American Modern Dancers is written for students of

dance and for all interested in dance arts and how they influence and are influenced by dancers and their audiences. One of the greatest American dancers, Martha Graham, has said: "A dancer's world is the heart of Man . . . The History of the dance is the social history of the world."

Dance has a dynamic image which may be experienced only through the participation of living dancers and living audiences. No book, painting nor sculptured frieze can make you *see* dance, for dance is an art with its own medium and aesthetics. It is impossible to convey one art through the medium of another. And the dance is psychical as well as physical; therefore, the audience at a dance performance and the reader of a book about dancing must accept the poetic or spiritual nature of dance while recognizing its kinetic substance: its form and expression as movement.

When writing and speaking about dancing it is sometimes necessary to make use of its terminology — the working vocabulary for the style of dance. The Modern Dance terminology used in this book is current and local in the United States, published in texts and manuals and in analytic books on the dance. In the past twenty years international dance arts have compiled a huge literary record, and city and college libraries in the United States now offer readers materials for research into dance and its related arts. Several of the dancers described in this book have written biographically and clinically about their lives and works, thus giving the reader the most personal and revealing literary accounts of Modern Dance.

This book is not a manual on Modern Dance, nor an analytical study of techniques and choreography for dance. It will not give lessons to the student nor help the teacher compose exercises in dance. It is not a thesis on dance, but a book about dancers.

It is confined to only a few dancers and describes some but not all of the major developments in Modern Dance. It omits a great deal of what is pertinent (as in academic aspects of the dance) and tries to avoid duplicating other books on the subject. As I have researched more from persons than from printed records this book has its bibliography in people, not in print. I have referred, by title and author, to certain books which should broaden the reader's understanding of the dancers and their styles.

The history of Modern Dance is important to every dance student, and it is equally important to students of music, painting and the arts of design, drama and all theatre arts, and sociology. Dance teachers and students made suggestions and recommendations for this book, and one chief requirement was for the Notes, which amplify some statements in the narrative. Another requirement was that this book place the dance within its eras, parallel with other trends in society and the arts, especially the arts of music and painting.

I acknowledge with gratitude a wealth of personal reminiscence by the dancers' contemporaries and their pupils. Hitherto unpublished statements about Isadora

Duncan are from private English papers, and I received help from Bruce King, who assisted with the Duncan archives at the New York Public Library. I am indebted to the Ted Shawn records for material on Denishawn and I gratefully acknowledge the help received through readings of portions of my manuscript by Martha Graham and Craig Barton, her assistant at the Martha Graham School of Contemporary Dance, by Elsa Rainer and Hanya Holm, and by Katherine Litz, named for me by Doris Humphrey as the authority on her work. My editor, Emilie W. McLeod, guided me in extracting the single volume from the enormous mass and varied detail of Modern Dance.

OLGA MAYNARD

California
Spring, 1964

Contents

❧ ❦

Illustrations

(between pages 110-111)

AMERICAN
MODERN DANCERS
The Pioneers

Introduction: A Definition

THE ARTS of a people are expressions of their spirit. National characteristics distinguish the ways in which peoples make music, sing and dance, and write poetry and drama. We know how the ancient Greeks thought and behaved, and how they looked in dress and gesture, but only because Greek poets and sculptors and painters preserved their memories for future men.

There are only two primary arts: the art of dancing and the art of building. And dancing came first. Dance is the oldest, noblest and most cogent of the arts, the source of all arts that express themselves first within the person. Music, drama and poetry are sister arts to dance. Architecture, or the art of building, is the second primary art, standing at the source of those arts that lie without the person. Sculpture, painting and the arts of design lie within the art of building. The two primary arts, dance and architecture, unite in the theatre to form those communicative expressions of creativity that we call theatrical arts.

Dancing is a primal impulse, older than mankind,

born of rhythm. The art of dancing was formed in pre-historic eras, for by the beginning of civilization the dance had already reached a degree of perfection which no other art or science attained for centuries thereafter. Primitive societies developed dance arts of an intricacy of design and difficulty of execution that compare with the most artistic dance creations of our time.

More than five hundred years before the birth of Christ, Confucius wrote that *a nation's character is typified by its dancers,* and that *one may judge a king by the state of dancing during his reign.* In the twentieth century Americans developed a style of dancing called "Modern," which, like jazz, exerted an extraordinary worldwide influence not only on the musical arts but also on social behavior.

Theatre represents entertainment to most audiences. But its origin was in more profound functions. The history of theatre began with the Greeks, and it is in their history that we seek the roots of theatre dance. "Theatre" was "a place to view" and the "doing place" was the dancing place. "Drama" comes from *dromenon:* a thing done, and in this Grecian concept of theatre there was no separation between the arts of dance, drama, music and poetry. All were combined and related in "Rhythmic Movement," born of a single instinct and common to humanity. Primitive man's dance was his science, art and religion. The earliest inspiration for theatre lies in man's awareness of a cycle of seasons and the drama of the universe. It is from this first savage awe that mankind conceived mood and climax for spectacle in theatre. And the Greeks' theatre, the "place to view" the expressions of artists, was drawn from their *dionysia*, the religious rite of dance by which they celebrated death-into-life, the immortality of the soul as symbolized in the birth of spring from the season of winter.

Theatre dance is separate in kind from dancing in the ballroom, the social form of dance, and from the dance of the village green, which we call "folk" dance. Theatre dance is not sacred dance, the dancing through which some societies worship deities. Primitive, ethnic, folk and all other kinds of dance must be specifically arranged for theatrical presentation before they can be accepted as staged dance for audiences.

Ballet is theatre dance for which the artists are professionally trained in a *technique* or art medium, toward certain dance *aesthetics*, a distinguishing quality or philosophy for this style of dancing. Ballet has a science for training the artist and an artistic standard which is its poetic ideal. It is internationally recognized as having a codified formula, or structure, dating from 1661.

The dance in America which is "Modern" is a kind of dance developed in the twentieth century, and it is labeled "Modern" because it is new or contemporary, of our times. This dance was not created scientifically, like ballet, on the human possibilities of movement in dance. It derived its form from spirit — the personal, intimate statements of dancers who did not use the known and recognized styles of dance, but invented a new phraseology, exactly as a writer would innovate a new style for a novel form of literature.

The originator of the twentieth-century dance was an American woman, Isadora Duncan, and her new dance had a zealousness and rapture of the spirit, with a physical expressiveness of great freedom. Duncan's dance was born, or created, out of her own rebellions against the conventions of dance and of society, and from her stated principles concerning the art of dancing. She was not a professional dancer with a technique for dance, and she said that her dance was not of the theatre, but an expression of life. According to her principles, her pupils were not trained for exhibition onstage. And yet Duncan danced in theatres, alone and with groups of her students, appearing on stages for audiences in America, England, Europe and Russia. Duncan placed on view in the twentieth-century theatre the new or Modern dance.

Ballet, from its inception, had formal structure or technique.[1]

Modern Dance was a spirit or philosophy from which the first, or pioneer, Modern dancers drew inspiration. The form or structure of Modern Dance as an art form developed gradually and from the personal principles of these pioneer dancers.

Modern Dance is a state of mind as much as a style of movement.

Ballet has characteristics of dance closely allied to architecture in line and balance, and a peculiar stance called "turn out" by which the dancer's feet copy the fencer's stance, a basis of the seventeenth-century dance. Ballet is architectural in form, as well as rhythmic in space. The ballet is concerned with solid geometry and human anatomy as well as a poetic concept for dance. The choreographer, the composer of dance, usually works in the form which was set down by the first choreographer in 1580, "a geometrical arrangement of numerous people dancing together under a diverse harmony of many instruments." [2] Ballet is comparable to grand opera in its use of orchestral music, scenic design, stage mechanics and libretti. The ballet dancer is subject to the choreographer, the composer of the ballet work, and performs according to a technique and within the aesthetics of the ballet art. This type of dancer, a trained artist in the oldest theatrical profession, is to be compared to the musical instrumentalist who performs the composer's music. The ballet dancer interprets the choreographer's intent and performs his design but does not seek to personally express his own thoughts and feelings about life.

Isadora Duncan's dance expressed her personal thought and feeling, and all succeeding creative Modern dancers have expressed theirs according to physique as well as temperament. For this reason, Modern Dance is an expression individual to its creators, and controversial as an art form. It is controversial because it is made up of the individual, and often contradictory, statements of its creators, each of whom was first an individual intelligence before becoming a contributing influence on the dance. One of these creators, Doris Humphrey, said that all Modern dancers are shouts to the world. It is the chorus of their voices, in the original statements they made, which express the dance called "Modern."

These dancers' states of minds, or their individual philosophies — ideas — were expressed in ways of movement, from which came the style of Modern Dance. The principles of Modern Dance — its *technique*, or system of training, and *aesthetics*, or artistic ideal — developed in the first part of the twentieth century through the work of American dancers with contributing influences from Central European Modern Dance. The twentieth-century dance developed in Europe parallel to but separate from American Modern Dance. Both drew their root source from Isadora Duncan.

Modern dancers began by dancing alone, sometimes without musical accompaniment — a dance of silence — sometimes to music which had not been intended for the dance. Modern Dance did not begin with geometrical design for choreography but as the improvisations of creative dancers. At first, it had no terminology except poetic statements which lacked concise definition. But for an art to exist it must have form; and no expression of creative thought has art form until it evolves a recognized medium of expression, a system of training by which its original performance may be re-created, and a structure which distinguishes its performance as being particular to the art. Modern Dance, therefore, had to discipline its rebellious character sufficiently to accept rules or principles which would give it form as well as spirit.

How Modern Dance began, and why, must be researched not only in the history of dancing but also in the social history of Western civilization. Isadora Duncan fancifully described herself as springing to life as a dancer like Athene from the head of Zeus, but the Modern Dance grew from wider and more profound influences in its times than out of a single gifted dancer. The stories of the creators of Modern Dance not only describe how they formed the style of dance but also explain how they were impelled to dance, for what purpose, and toward what ends. Their ideas, freely expressed in dance, are the basis for the "controlled freedom" of the present art form.

The most romantic and paradoxical fact about Modern Dance is that it began as a rebellion against the social and artistic conventions of the times, and became the chief style of creative dance in America. It was denounced as non-art in form, and as immoral because of its "free" style, but it became the academic American dance, a part of the normal educational curriculum.

Modern Dance has remained controversial in the theatre. Its idiom or style remains dependent on the creativity of the individual dancer. Its first fiercely creative period was called "days of divine indiscipline," but it eventually achieved a recognized system by which its methods are now taught, and a formal structure composed of elements named dynamism, metakinesis, substance and form.[3]

Modern Dance never succeeded in commanding the international theatre as did ballet. Its academic basis is now almost entirely centered in the United States, and American dancers exert worldwide influences. Pure works of Modern Dance are generally accepted as being of intellectual interest rather than entertainment.

Modern Dance has significantly influenced the ballet not only in the United States but throughout the international theatre. Some of the most revolutionary developments in classical dance of the twentieth century are directly reflective of principles of movement and of philosophies in art originally explored by Modern dancers.

And Modern Dance is the basis of rhythmic movement in American education. Every woman's college of note and almost every university incorporates Modern Dance in its curriculum, either as physical education or as fine arts.

The physical aspects of Modern Dance are stressed in elementary and high school education, in youth and adult community centers, and in summer camps. Modern Dance is the accepted system of movement for education and recreation because it adapts to physical exercise and artistic creativity. What began as the zealous personal expression of a few individuals, each working alone in search of means of communicating the inner self, has become the general property of the majority and for a variety of uses. Modern Dance is the American dance because we inaugurated it, developed it, and because we have made the most ordinary and extraordinary uses of it, thereby proving what Isadora Duncan wished to teach: that the dance is not outside life, but of life itself.

The styles that were new and strange at the beginning of the century are now known and ordinary to the dance, and the title "Modern" no longer literally applies to its forms. For lack of a more vital and universal title this label continues to identify the dance which is not ballet or ethnic or folk.

To the uninformed, Modern Dance remains eccentric and esoteric. But, in fact, it is a dance that is organic and expressive of the contemporary dancers — a dance of experience shared between dancers and their audiences.

❧ I ❧

The Beginnings

Isadora Duncan is considered the first of the American Modern dancers, the wellspring of Modern Dance. But Duncan might never have been inspired to dance without influences which came to her from such diverse sources as archaeological science[4] and the theories inaugurated by François Delsarte, Friedrich Froebel, and Sigmund Freud.

Duncan and the dance of the twentieth century were shaped by influences older than the eras which developed them, and from far wider sources than those in America. The entire nature of dance was reanalyzed in Duncan's time, and the most striking changes in technical methods and artistic meanings came from Delsarte and Emile Jacques-Dalcroze, who were not dancers. In some respects, Freud, a medical scientist, influenced twentieth-century arts as much as the creative artists. The "age of Freud" in the first part of the century was as revolutionary for society and culture as the "age of the atom" has become in our era.[5]

Duncan was not alone, nor was she the first to explore

dance for a deeper meaning than entertainment and in a more natural style than the one conventional to the nineteenth-century theatre dance. Before Duncan, and parallel with her, dancers strove for methods of expression and communication strange to the mode of their times, but remarkably close to the ancient Grecian ideal for dancing.

Duncan might never have been encouraged to dance as a child if Froebel's theories for education had not been accepted in American society. He was the innovator of the kindergarten and the training of women as teachers, and he believed that children should be taught along lines of natural growth and not in a set formula for thought and behavior. He also urged the teaching of rhythmic movement and creative play for the development of a harmonious body and mind.[6] From about 1800 his theories were accepted in America, and dance as physical exercise gained popularity. Froebel's theories prepared the American school system for the physical education curriculums we know today. And they so affected Duncan's era that in her childhood middle-class Americans already accepted the dance as a means of healthy exercise. Dancing lessons were as commonplace as lessons on the piano in the parlor.

New in Duncan's youth was a mode called "Delsartian," which affected the theatre and the arts in Europe and, thereafter, in America. Its style was humanistic rather than formal. Nineteenth-century ideals of artistic beauty were as rigid as the modes in dress fashion and social manners. The nice or approved norm in theatre was an elaborate stereotype where gesture was stylized rather than normally expressive. There was a marked difference between the gesture of the street and gesture onstage.

Delsarte was a French teacher of music who was the first to make a scientific analysis of gesture and emotional expression. His theories on the expressional capacity of the body in zones of intellect, emotion and physique and in relation to space, motion and time had great influence on the graphic arts. Radical changes in the name of "naturalness" affected the theatre.

Many of these changes came directly and indirectly from Freudian theories concerning the mind and the person. Freud's theories and findings in psychoanalysis were applied to anthropology, sociology, child development, religion, politics and the arts. Psychoanalysis scientifically supported older theories, some of them anticipated intuitively by Arthur Schopenhauer, which prescribed the free thought and new behavior patterns of the twentieth century.

The importance of recognition of the inner self in relation to the outer self and society is the Freudian thesis. It is also the thesis of Modern Dance. Freudian science stimulated the arts to interpret reality in bolder and freer terms than had been the mode. Duncan and dance were not solitary or isolated in the revolutionary times in which they developed. Duncan's times (1878-1927) coincide with those of the Norwegian dramatist Henrik

Ibsen (1828-1906), with whom modern drama began. By stripping from his plays anything that was artificial or melodramatic this playwright introduced realism and human psychological meanings into theatre. Ibsen in drama worked toward the same truth and naturalness the Moderns sought to express in dancing. New ideas and new techniques, alterations in the formal structure of the stage drama and the novel gave birth to a new literary style. "Veritism" and the minute recordings of human consciousness, the presentation of psychological experience as analytically as the description of physical incidents, were developed with variations in the writings of Henry James, Romain Rolland, Marcel Proust, D. H. Lawrence, Virginia Woolf and James Joyce. Realism at its starkest and most pitiless was promoted in fiction writing by Theodore Dreiser, Sinclair Lewis, Sherwood Anderson, Ernest Hemingway, William Faulkner and others. Parallel trends in all the arts may be traced through succeeding eras.[7]

These current influences were most vividly recognized in music, dance and painting, because of the audiovisual nature of the arts. The innovations in ballet music showed a striking change between the nineteenth and twentieth centuries. These are best understood by listening to romantic dance music like Tchaikovsky's three ballet masterpieces, *Swan Lake, The Sleeping Beauty* and *The Nutcracker,* and comparing their form and style with Stravinsky's ballet music, as *The Rite of Spring, Petrouchka* and *Renard.*[8] Painting, especially the French school, received succeeding shock waves of thought and passed rapidly through a succession of revolutions in technique and artistic tastes.

The rebels in music and painting aroused audience and critical response as varied as that which reacted to Modern Dance. Duncan's detractors resisted her rebellion against conventional theatre dance and called her style of dancing formless and immoral. Meanwhile, those who resisted the sweeping changes in music and painting described the "modern" artists in these media as madmen and wild beasts.[9]

It was not a peculiarity of Duncan to insist on naturalness as preferable to stylization. The world, especially that of the Western cultures, was in the throes of a gigantic spasm of artistic creativity which matched and perhaps exceeded the shifting values and standards of society in industry, economics and class consciousness. From these great social and scientific upheavals came a new basis for thought and behavior, and for the public taste in art. What had been damned was praised, while that which had stood as the model became outdated. In the many raging controversies of the times that of the Modern Dance was only one. But it was one which would defy a wholly objective analysis, or a settlement in the artistic sense, of the arguments over its form as art.

✍ Delsarte

François Delsarte (1811-1871) studied singing and acting at the Paris Conservatoire of Music. His voice was ruined by faulty teaching based on the then accepted methods of forcing the student into a mode or mold, regardless of personal or individual limitations and capacities. He remained in the theatre as a supernumerary and devoted his life to formulating laws of expression as guides for principles of art.

He first researched diligently the ways in which human beings of all ages, temperaments, and social classes reacted physically to emotions of every sort. His investigations were of the world at large, ranging from children and their nurses in city parks to a mine disaster where he observed the behavior of the rescue squads and the victims' friends and relatives. Attitudes, gestures, tones of voice and manners of speech were catalogued. He underwent a course of medical study in order to know anatomy, and he worked in one of the terrible madhouses of his time to gain knowledge of the insane. Human beings of every aspect of feeling in life and death, normal and abnormal, were clinically observed for his summations of how people behave in various circumstances, and how they express their thoughts and emotions.

From about 1839 Delsarte began to teach his "laws of expression" to artists in the theatre and also to painters, sculptors and composers, lawyers, statesmen and clergymen. His "Science of Applied Aesthetics" divided movement into eccentric, concentric and normal, with rules by which the body could be controlled to express the thought and feeling of the person within a characterization and true to a time and place. In short, his principles were for the liveliest interpretation of human intellect and emotion, of a realism and profundity the theatre had not yet experienced.

"Delsartian" ideals influenced the graphic and plastic arts, vocal and instrumental music, acting and oratory. And dance, in which Delsarte had no active participation whatever, benefited most from his principles for human movement expressive of the inner human self.

In the American Modern Dance two streams of influence descend from Delsarte: one Duncan's, received by her through vague currents and nameless sources, and the other from Americans who are known to have studied Delsartian science of applied aesthetics. One such was Genevieve Stebbins, who traveled to Europe and studied Delsarte's theories from his pupils, protégés taught by the master during his lifetime. Before Isadora Duncan's appearance as a dancer in 1895, Mrs. Stebbins was a well-known performer of "modern" or new style in dance. She studied antique art in Europe and formulated dance movement based on Greek statuary and Renaissance painting. Mrs. Stebbins was one of several dancers who, before Duncan, practiced a new mode of "interpretative" dance, influenced by Delsartian principles of expressiveness.

Delsarte's students included the singer Jenny Lind; Bizet, the composer of the opera *Carmen*; and Rachel, the great tragedienne of the French theatre. His influence affected the art of William Charles Macready, the great English "King Lear" of Edwin Booth's era. Delsartian principles were widespread in the theatre into which Isadora Duncan adventured in the last decade of the nineteenth century.

Delsartian influence on dance can be traced through Duncan, Ruth St. Denis and Ted Shawn, and the European Modern dancer Kurt Jooss, who received this influence from Rudolf von Laban. Delsartian principles penetrate the techniques of Martha Graham and Doris Humphrey; Graham's "contraction and release" and Humphrey's "fall and recovery" are applications of Delsartian theories. These were adopted in the German Modern Dance as *spannung* in *anspannung* and *abspannung*, tension to its zenith, relaxation to its nadir, as formulated by Delsarte in his "laws" of Reaction, Recoil, etc.[10]

His "Law of Velocity," i.e., the slowness or quickness of movement in ratio to the mass (weight) moved and the distance in space through which it is moved, is based on the pendulum. Its applications within dance developed new concepts of movement in ratio to space.

✍ Dalcroze

Emile Jacques-Dalcroze (1865-1950) was a Swiss music teacher who evolved a system, Eurhythmics, and established a method of teaching coordination of music and bodily movement. He founded institutes in Germany and England, and similiar schools were started in Paris, Vienna, Stockholm, and several other cities. Eurhythmics is now the indispensable primary education of the young dancer, because it teaches the exact interpretation into movement of the time and the intervals of music for dancing. Dalcroze's stated intent was "to create by the help of a rhythm a rapid and regular current of communication between brain and body, and to make feeling for rhythm a physical experience." He felt that his work was indebted to Duncan's dance, but she herself rejected his systematic and analytic dance as being too mechanical. Nevertheless, Dalcroze had a profound and far-reaching influence on dance.

Dalcroze's celebrated pupils were Mary Wigman, the genius of German Modern Dance, and Marie Rambert, the initial and most original influence in English ballet. Wigman's principles passed directly from her to her pupils in her German *schule* system of training. Rambert, a teacher and an impresario, founded a school and maintained a theatre, the famous Mercury in London.[11] Two of Rambert's students were Antony Tudor and Agnes de Mille.

The influences of Delsarte and Dalcroze on dance are accepted. The degrees of influence, and through which channels these influences affect ballet and Modern Dance, are still debated. They cause considerable argument, as do the precise extent and points of influences of the German on the American Modern Dance.

✍ German Modern Dance

German dance of the twentieth century, also called Central European dance, was founded on the theory and analysis of Rudolf von Laban (1879-1958), a Hungarian teacher who worked in Germany until the Nazi regime drove him to England. His influence is generally acknowledged in the continental and the American dance, and his system of dance notation, Labanotation, is widely used.

Laban elaborated a precise analysis and a philosophy for the dance, based on typing dancers in much the way that singers are typed for characteristics as sopranos and contraltos, tenors and baritones.[12] Laban studied under a Delsarte disciple and was trained in ballet technique. After a world tour he became deeply affected by the ecstatic nature of Asian religious dance. Two of his pupils were Mary Wigman and Kurt Jooss.[13] Another of his protégés was Harald Kreutzberg.[14] Kreutzberg was active as a performer in the United States during the 1930s, and exerted influences of his own. José Limón began to study dance after seeing a performance by Kreutzberg in New York.

The Germans called their twentieth-century dance "expressionistic." Impressions or expressions of German dance began to influence American dancers in the 1920s, but its formal structure as dance was not recognized until authorized Wigman teachers arrived in the United States.

Twentieth-century dance had moved far from the concepts of form and interpretation traditional to ballet. Its tenet was freedom, a rebellion from formality. The new styles and techniques began to be codified into systems for training dancers, and the dance revolution entered a period of reform. The Germans led the scientific and mathematical approach to the "new" dance with scholarly treatises and analyses.

In America dancers continued to be independently resourceful rather than scientific and disciplined. The great American Modern dancers were autonomous. But the first academy of dance was established in 1914, a school and company founded by the American dancers Ruth St. Denis and Ted Shawn which existed until 1932. The eclectic dance curriculum at Denishawn stretched back to primitive forms and advanced boldly into Music Visualizations. It extended geographically and historically by introducing the Oriental dance styles in which St. Denis excelled and Shawn's dances of the North and South American continent, ancient Crete, India and Japan.

Ted Shawn, who is encyclopedically referred to as "the father of American Dance," innovated approaches to dance based on physical and psychical impulses and responses that were natural and distinctive to men. They were essentially masculine in form and feeling, differing from dance which was essentially of a feminine character. His sense of the *gender of the dance* heightened its drama.

The first concrete German influences on American Modern Dance began with the importation to Denishawn of a Wigman pupil, Margaret Wallman. In 1930 Shawn went to Germany to dance a repertoire of his solos, including *Prometheus Bound*.[15] The premiere concert was marked by anti-American demonstrations by university students of the post-World War I generation but at the end of the concert the audience gave Shawn a standing ovation. The Germans thereafter lionized him. Their greatest sculptor, George Kolbe, took Shawn as a model (calling him the most wonderful male model he had ever known), and a noted art critic, Katherine S. Dreier, wrote a study: *Shawn, The Dancer*. Shawn was invited to participate in the Third German Dance Congress in Munich, to star in the title role of Wallman's *Orpheus-Dionysus*.

Wallman had danced in Wigman's company and directed the Wigman-Schule, from which she had drawn a group, Tanzer-Collectif-1930 (Dance Group 1930), to dance at the Munich Congress. Half aggressively, the German dancers described to Shawn the developments

German dance had made under Wigman. Shawn retorted by showing them works in print which supported his claim that American dancers had, in many instances, already passed beyond these.

Friendly rivalry worked in an exchange program. Shawn danced and taught in Germany and invited Wallman to America to teach at Denishawn, where she arrived in 1931. Wallman taught the principles of Wigman's system, and German technique entered the curriculum at Denishawn, taking its place amiably among every other form of dance from hula to ballet.

Wallman was an experienced and gifted teacher, and (according to Shawn) a creative and imaginative artist. She was afterwards choreographer for the Vienna Opera and the Teatro Colón in Buenos Aires. A well-known opera director, she has done work in America as recently as 1960, for the Chicago Opera, and in 1964 for the New York Metropolitan Opera.

But Shawn remained untouched by German dance, and St. Denis described it as "sadly earthbound." It was not Wallman but a later German dancer, Hanya Holm, who made a permanent impression on American Modern dance forms. Holm, too, was Wigman-trained and an authorized Wigman System teacher. She settled in the United States in the creative period of the dance and became one of its pioneer forces. Another Wigman pupil, Pola Nirenska, worked in Washington, D. C.

⤧ *Mary Wigman*

Born in Hanover in 1886, Mary Wigman studied under Dalcroze and Laban and then broke away from her mentors to develop some original concepts. From 1924 she stood as the genius of German dance. The commonest terms associated with her work are "dance without music," "tension-relaxation," "space" and "expressionistic dance." Above all, she emphasized the dynamic form in the dance, dance as movement alone. For this the phrase "absolute dance" was coined, but it did not mean that the dance was ultimate or perfect, only that it was absolute as dance. In *The Book of the Dance* (1963) Agnes de Mille describes Wigman as being "fascinated by movement as organic pattern, the development of visual conclusions and enlargements from single gestures or simple phrases of gesture." Wigman was the first to analyze movement and use its elements in treatments, developments and variations as a musical composer uses notes to produce melody and harmony. Her theses remain extraordinarily valid and vital to contemporary dance. She still teaches in Germany, and in 1964 visited the United States.

Both American and German dance based structure on natural movements. In order to emphasize *movement as the substance of dance* Wigman composed dancing without music. Later, she made use of percussive accompaniment. The German dance's character was subjective and expressionistic, and the Germans analyzed and qualified dancing with a scientific detachment as well as an aesthetic involvement.

Twentieth-century German dance owed much of its character and spirit to Delsarte and Isadora Duncan. It was strongly affected by the scientific theories of Dalcroze and Laban, and had been enriched by the art of Ruth St. Denis in the prewar period of her European tours. The Germans called St. Denis the "hieratic dancer," and the tight form of her dance *geschlossen*. St. Denis, like Duncan, rebelled against formality in dance. She possessed an unbelievable control of her body. Her "rippling arms," as in *The Cobras*, so discernibly rippled that doctors of anatomy in Europe sought her backstage and begged to be allowed to examine her arms for a scientific explanation of their phenomenal muscular control.

Wigman was concerned with space, an obsession which characterized Western culture artistically and scientifically. Duncan had only begun to explore its possibilities for Modern Dance with her insistence on natural movement — movement not prescribed by codified dance but emergent from the human body, in normal or spontaneous gesture in relation to time, rhythm and space.

Wigman's dynamic principles for dance were scientifically as well as brilliantly expressed, and she explained the dance as rising, in construction, from the dancer's experience. She saw each dancer as carrying his own and characteristic theme. "The experience shapes the kernel, the basic accord of . . . dance existence around which all else crystallizes." Wigman's choreography and her system for teaching were based on her premise of the "dance of experience."

The German dancer was the artist of a certain nation and a particular era, affected by the disillusionment and suffering of a defeated Germany in the postwar period. Contrarily, the American Modern Dance began with the joyous expression of the Dionysiac Isadora Duncan and the romantic Ruth St. Denis. Ted Shawn, the first male to be described as "dancer" in the United States population census, used dance as a language of movement to express the ideas of all manner of peoples and places. It was "world dance" rather than the image in dance of *his* person and *his* place.

Hanya Holm, comparing the American and the German Modern dancers, found that the American dancer tended to observe, portray and comment on his surroundings with insight mainly through intellect and analysis. The German dancer began with emotional experience and its effect on the individual. The overall study of every aspect of Modern Dance, in the repertoires and teaching systems of every major dancer, reveals the seesaw between these two poles, which often meet and dissolve in one work.

The systematic developments of German Modern Dance were especially important in the use of space, but it would be unwise to state arbitrarily that this was solely and exclusively a German development. For while Wigman was asking theoretic questions of her work, parallel developments established spatial precepts under a variety of terms in American dance.

The purpose of bodily movement to express the dancer's emotional and mental attitudes was the great attribute of Modern Dance. In this, Wigman's "dance of experience" was a major development. The composition of large-scale dramatic works for groups of dancers was perfected by the Americans, notably by Doris Humphrey. Thus it was in America that Modern Dance moved from a small arena of personal experience, a chamber-sized art form, into the more majestic proportions of theatre art. The later repertoires of Martha Graham and Doris Humphrey and some of José Limón's rank with great operas and dramas. For some intellectuals, these Modern Dance works far exceed in importance anything in the twentieth-century ballet.

Modern Dance began its intuitive and inspirational phase in Isadora. It developed technically and analytically with the work of three Denishawn dancers, Martha Graham, Doris Humphrey and Charles Weidman, and with Hanya Holm, the German dancer who settled in America in 1931.

The 1930s were the fruition period for Modern Dance. Isadora's seeds of inspiration had found the fertile ground and equable climate of Denishawn. There grew the roots of genius in Graham and Humphrey. Since then it has flowered, put down new seeds and thrived on some foreign grafts until the American Modern Dance heritage resembles a great, burgeoning "family tree." To this tree, every student belongs by right of the dancer's traditions.

By the end of the Second World War, American dancers rose to the front rank of the international dance theatre. When normal traffic between nations was resumed in the late 1940s and the 1950s it was recognized that American Modern dancers led the field. A vital and luminous force was felt worldwide in the dance and much of it stemmed from that style of dancing Europeans had, at first, called "the American dance."

Isadora Duncan was not the first American dancer to appear in Europe. Loie Fuller, an Illinois-born performer called "The Star from the West," was famous before Isadora. And even before Fuller, an American had awed and enchanted the European audience. In the early 1800s, the heyday of the ballerinas Marie Taglioni and Fanny Elssler, a fifteen-year-old dancer from Philadelphia, Augusta Maywood, caused a sensation at the Paris Opéra and then became a prima ballerina who ranked with the great Elssler.

Fuller is largely overlooked by Americans, but she was a famous artiste in Europe, where she had her own company and a theatre in Paris. She innovated stage lighting, machinery and effects that helped to revolutionize the century's theatre. And it was Fuller, a remarkably generous artist, who arranged Isadora's debut in Vienna. Fuller also befriended another well-known dancer of the day, Canadian-born, California-reared Maud Allan.[16]

Allan greatly resembled Isadora in style and in the use of great music for the "interpretive" dance. She was the unrivaled Salome, prototype of innumerable seductive Oriental heroines in the dance.

Yet it is not with Fuller nor with Allan that the American Modern Dance is identified, but with Isadora. And it is with this beautiful rebel's story that the history of the twentieth-century dance begins.

✍ *Isadora Duncan: The Seed of Inspiration*

Dora Angela Duncan was born May 27, 1878, in San Francisco, California. She was the youngest of four children in an Irish-American family. Her mother, Mary Dora Gray, was of good family and had been a piano teacher before her marriage to a widower considerably her senior, a banker named Joseph Charles Duncan.

Joseph Duncan was tried four times in court for embezzlement; however, each time he was acquitted. When his wife was expecting their fourth child he deserted her. The child was born fatherless but to an incredible destiny.

Isadora went to England and Europe as a poor unknown young American dancer and became the Pied Piper of her era, leading the rich, the intellectual and the artistic of society in her train. She danced through Europe and Russia and made an impression more as a prophet than as a dancer. Isadora not only changed the history of dance but also audiences' ideas about dancing.

After Isadora, the dance was not simply a technical mastery over difficult combinations of movements but a cult for the intelligentsia and an art expression which aesthetically ranked with poetry and music.

Isadora changed theatre dance costume and style. After her, dancers (including those of the ballet) wore appropriate rather than stylized dress for dancing, and their gestures were natural instead of stilted in a stage formula grown stale and rigid.

The wonder is that Isadora accomplished these things. She did not have a great intellect, yet she convinced intellectuals. She was not a trained dancer, yet she dictated a new way of dancing. As the Duncan legend formed, it partially concealed the secret of Isadora's power. Isadora believed that she had been born to dance Beauty back into the world.

"I belong to the Gods," Isadora wrote of herself. "My life is ruled by signs and portents, which I follow to my set goals."

The "gods" of which she spoke so intimately were those of Greek myth, from whom Isadora earnestly believed herself descended. She said that she sprang to life full-grown as a dancer, like Athene from the head of Zeus, and she believed that she was a mortal incarnation of Aphrodite, who bade her to dedicate herself to Dionysus. As a young girl, before she carried her dreams into reality, Isadora wrote a passionate invocation to the pagan gods, calling on Athene, Pan, and Terpsichore to help her to dance better and in their honor.

Sworn to a worship of these gods, Isadora danced with a Dionysian fervor and uttered oracular statements not only about the art of dancing but also about life and love. All her actions, and the success she enjoyed, are explained by understanding that Isadora believed herself to be an extraordinary being with extraordinary powers; dedicated and destined to her way of life. With this invincible belief Isadora journeyed far from home, rose to dizzy heights of fame, was hailed as the great revolutionary and major prophet of her time — and changed, even into our time, the dance of theatre, concert hall, and school and university.

We do not know when or why she changed her given name Dora to Isadora. But changing names was a family habit, one of the exercises of the Duncan imagination. Dora was given the pet name "Dorita." The elder Duncan children were named Mary Elizabeth, known for part of her life as May; Augustine and Raymond. In the legend of Isadora Duncan, her sister and brothers are known as Elizabeth, Augustin, and Raymond. There were no others of that generation, although the use by writers of Elizabeth's other names has misled readers into the belief that Isadora had more than one sister. All the other Duncans pale into insignificance beside the incandescent fame of the youngest.

Isadora's whole life and career were strongly influenced by early impressions and familial interests. Mrs. Duncan was musical, poetic and intensely religious, and all the children were theatrically inclined. Music, drama and mysticism as well as poverty and hardship were the sum of Isadora's childhood. She grew up in a broken home, petted by her older sister and brothers as the baby born "after Papa deserted us." Mrs. Duncan was an embittered woman who did not spare her children the sordid details of her unhappy marriage. It is notable that Elizabeth Duncan never married, that Isadora made a pact in her girlhood never to "subjugate" herself to a man, and that she did not marry until she was middle-aged and well entrenched in her chosen career as a dancer.

Isadora was a rebel, and her revolution was not only against the ballet but also against her era's ideas about men and women. The woman suffrage movement, begun in the United States in mid-century, was by then sweeping women to the resolution that standards applied equally for men and women. The century which produced Susan B. Anthony and Julia Ward Howe was the era of Isadora and her "new" ideal for dance. With the zeal typical of her time, Isadora set out to change the world she lived in.

She danced as soon as she walked, making up dances while her mother played the piano and her sister and brothers recited poetry. The Duncans lived alternately in San Francisco and Oakland, and Mrs. Duncan supported the family by giving piano lessons and knitting. She was devoted to her handsome, talented children. Isadora never forgot her childhood memory of falling asleep and seeing her mother working at a piece of knitting that had to be delivered at a certain time, and waking the next morning to see Mrs. Duncan crouched over the work, daylight dimming the lamp that had burned all night. The Duncan children were sometimes sent door to door in the city to sell samples of their mother's knitting and "Dorita" had the most success, because she was a pretty little girl with winning ways.

Beauty and charm and the serene belief that she was a special person were Isadora's gifts from birth. As she grew up, she assumed that she was destined to be a great woman. Her first memory was of being thrown from the window of a burning house. It was the beginning of the glare of notoriety in which she lived and died.

The precocious child danced with such grace and authority that at the age of six she was teaching neighborhood children, who paid her with pennies begged from their mothers. Mrs. Duncan sent her to a ballet teacher, but he was no match for the strong-willed little girl. Isadora refused to study the classical dance because she found it too constricting in its principles. She informed her family that she intended to compose a new way of dancing, one harmonious with Nature, borrowed from the ocean and the wind. To devote herself to this important work, she refused to go to school any longer. Isadora had little formal education and no dance training. But she had been born to dance, and what might have been the ruin of another child was the making of the dancer Isadora.

One of the major influences on her was that of a librarian, Ina Donna Coolbrith, who knew Joseph Duncan and took a personal interest in his daughter. Duncan had been a suitor of Miss Coolbrith's before marrying Isadora's mother, and while Mrs. Duncan described her husband as a scoundrel, Miss Coolbrith saw him in a more kindly light, and as a fellow-poet. Ina Coolbrith was a poetess of local note and the friend of two prominent writers, Bret Harte and Mark Twain. A spinster, she was remarkably well-educated and emancipated for her times. She was instrumental in having some of Joseph Duncan's verse included in a Bret Harte anthology in 1866, and she encouraged Dora Angela Duncan to read the works of great philosophers and poets. Literature opened up to the imaginative little girl a realm of romance and drama, peopled by powerful gods and heroic mortals. Myths became more important than reality. It was in the Oakland Library that Isadora Duncan began to dream of becoming the greatest dancer in the world.

The Duncans were theatre-mad, like many other Californians who generously spent money to import great theatrical stars to the "Wild West." Touring companies from Europe appeared regularly in San Francisco, and the young Duncans saw and loved England's greatest living actor, Henry Irving, and his leading lady, Ellen Terry. In the wake of the internationally famed, innumerable local artistes pursued careers, and one of the most popular forms of entertainment was "Harmonic Gymnastics" in the Delsartian mode.

The American actor Steele MacKaye, Delsarte's student in Europe, brought Delsarte's theories to the United

States and taught them in a course of "Harmonic Gymnastics" in his New York School of Expression. Delsarte did not teach his theories to dancers, but his applied aesthetics were put to use for dance, and MacKaye's harmonic gymnastics was a popular and influential version of the Delsartian theories.

Students from MacKaye's New York school derived the Delsartian principles from a source only once removed from their originator, and it may be assumed that they taught these harmonic gymnastics with authority. Certainly, the "Professors of Delsarte," as they called themselves, had an immediate effect on Americans, and the human element of Delsartian ideals became the vogue for "naturalness" in gesture and dress. The vogue for Delsarte ranged from a way of moving to a style in ladies' corsets. MacKaye, incidentally, was an actor-director, producer and playwright, thus exerting a fourfold influence on the theatre.

Another popular dance of the time was Neo-Grecian in style, so-called because the dancers wore copies of Greek dress and affected postures from Grecian statuary and etching. No one knows how the Greeks danced, but Greek artists of the centuries 7 through 4 B.C. left such lively imprints in the figures of dancers that it required little imagination for dancers to pose and gesture in a Neo-Grecian style. To accentuate the resemblance to antique statuary, some Neo-Grecian dancers whitened their skins for the look of marble. This was the opposite of the natural, human look, but Neo-Grecian dance merged with

"Harmonic Gymnastics" in the American dancers' repertoires.

Other entertainments featured elocution and mime. English pantomime, rich in expression, was often described in texts illustrated by pictures of well-known pieces of statuary, called "Grammars of Pantomime." Isadora owned a Grammar, and studied it as a source for her early work. She was greatly indebted to the art of pantomime in her theories of the new dance.

She never played at dancing, for while girls her age were dallying with floured faces and classical draperies, Isadora Duncan was earning a living. At fourteen, she was teaching the popular dances of the day — polka, schottische, mazurka, waltz — to pupils twice her age.

Joseph Duncan, married for the third time, had a fit of paternal responsibility and bought a mansion for his estranged family at the corner of Sutton and Van Ness streets in San Francisco. Here the young Duncans taught dancing and elocution, Mrs. Duncan presiding at the piano. For entertainment they staged amateur plays in the empty carriage house, where they could not afford to keep a carriage and pair.

Isadora, as remembered by her contemporaries, was at that time a pretty, imperious girl, not at all put out by the fact that she was from a family of poor "Irishers" and far, far removed from Nob Hill. She had done as she pleased from childhood, quitting school because she felt she must give all her life to making up dances. Her impressions and influences continued to come thick and fast, eagerly absorbed and mysteriously digested for her own creative instinct. Mrs. Duncan studied the Delsartian method, which was in reality MacKaye's version of applied aesthetics, and Isadora was sufficiently influenced by this method to style herself "Professor of Delsarte" on printed cards. She must have taken to heart Delsarte's thesis: "Gesture is the agent of the heart . . . of the soul . . . gesture is the spirit, of which speech is merely the letter." In later years, Isadora stressed in her teaching that the dancer must always first feel the movement within or the gestures would resemble the jerking of a puppet. Her audiences emphasized the "abandonment" of Duncan's dancing, but she taught her students that the emotions must always be more intense within than actually expressed through movement. The complete abandon which she advocated was to the gesture before attempting to perform it. These principles of a technique link Isadora's work with Delsartian principles far more closely than with Greek dance, which may well have been as formal as the ballet!

Isadora was not one of the Neo-Greek dancers; instead, she was experimenting with "natural rhythms." She had observed these in the sea, beside which she lived from childhood, and she connected this rhythm to her own bodily rhythm, the inhalation and exhalation of breath. However, she did not pursue this into scientific formula and intellectual thought; she simply used it from an instinctive emotional response. She was primarily moved by Beauty in the ideal of the human body, and the expression of the body in movement and in repose.

Her early dances were of *tableau vivant* form, rather like a game of statues come to life. She realized that soft and pliant material worn as costume added to the expressiveness of gesture and the drama of pose, and she designed draperies and dresses to suit her requirements. She was fond of blue, believing it was her supernatural "aura," or spiritual color, so she dyed her materials a particular shade of blue and copied it for curtains and backdrops. Adopting the Grecian sandal and sometimes discarding shoes altogether, she danced on a carpet, which lent the resilience she wished to find underfoot. As for the dances themselves, they were "natural" rhythms, governed only by what she felt *within* and allowed spontaneously to emerge. She stimulated her feeling for these rhythms with music and the recitation of verse. This early dancing was largely improvisation, and she explained it by terms like "collect one-self," and "continuous movement," which she believed allied to the gravitational force of the earth. The seat of the dancer's impulse she placed in the solar plexus, and described dance as the expression of a natural, inner urge.

When she was seventeen, and at a time when ladies scarcely ventured out of doors without male escort, Isadora took her mother to Chicago with the intention of earning a living by dancing.

She carried a letter of introduction to the Press Club of

Chicago from the San Francisco Press Club, for whose members Isadora had performed her artless "natural" dances. Charles Fair, a vaudeville manager, gave her a job at the Chicago Masonic Roof Garden and billed her as "The California Faun." Isadora became the pet of a club of Chicago writers, actors, painters and musicians who called themselves "Old Bohemia." Her simplicity and grace were appealing, and she enjoyed a success.

The impresario Charles Daly was urged to see the little "California Faun" who disported winningly in home-made muslin garments, "lightly as a zephyr and pliantly as a willow wand." Daly hired her on the spot for a New York revue where he billed her as "Sara Duncan." Here she made her first enemy, Mlle June May, a celebrated French mime, who was the star of the revue *Miss Pygmalion.*

When Mlle May complained to Daly that his protégée lacked any technical knowledge of dance and would ruin the show, Daly sent Isadora to study ballet with an Italian ballerina, Marie Bonfanti. Studying under Bonfanti did not alter Isadora's opinions about ballet, and she clung to her "natural" style. During rehearsals, when Isadora made a mistake Mlle May would pounce on her and pinch and slap her, but Daly kept Isadora and put her in several of his shows, including his production of *A Midsummer Night's Dream.* In those days, dancers were poorly paid and received no wages for rehearsal time. The Duncans eked out a bare existence on Isadora's tiny salary and by selling family ornaments.

Isadora's fortune took a turn for the better when she was discovered by New York society and engaged to perform at soirées, the private parties then in vogue at which theatre performers were the attractions. She was soon earning enough to bring the rest of the family to New York. The Duncans forsook their native California and the ill repute which had clung to their name from Joseph Duncan. With Mrs. Duncan as pianist, Elizabeth opened a dancing school at Carnegie Hall which proved so successful that it was moved to larger quarters at the Hotel Windsor on fashionable Fifth Avenue.

In 1897, when she was eighteen, Isadora went to England in Daly's company and he sent her to study ballet under Katti Lanner, a Viennese ballet mistress who was the choreographer and ballet mistress of London's famous Empire Theatre.[17] On her return to New York, Isadora returned to Bonfanti for lessons. Although Duncan continued to oppose the ballet as expressionless, it is a fact that she had preliminary ballet training.

Contrary to popular belief, Isadora Duncan did not improvise her dance onstage. She prepared very carefully, down to the least detail of drapery for clothing and background. It was her talent and her intention for her dance to appear artless. Many of her dances were rapturous to the point of abandon, but she worked from a dancer's discipline — and this she in part owed to her basic knowledge of ballet, which was then the only technical form of dancing other than the folk patterns of dance.

Encouraged by her admirers in New York and thwarted

by the work she was forced to perform onstage, Isadora's convictions that she must throw aside all conventions in order to compose her free, new dance were strengthened. Mlle May, for all her fame, seemed clumsy and insipid to Isadora — who, with characteristic lack of tact, did not hesitate to say so! Everything danced on the stage was put on to astonish the audience as a spectacle. But Isadora longed to touch the audience's soul with the power of dance. Epic thoughts from the great philosophers, muddled by indiscriminate reading and her own ardent dreams, stirred her to visions of herself as a prophet not only for the dance, but also for a way of thought and a way of life. "Freedom" was the key word of her prophecy, and "Beauty" was freedom's purpose and end. She knew of no better way, no other way, to convey her passionate beliefs than to relate them to the Greeks' mythological gods and goddesses and to express them through the symbolical Muses. There can be no doubt that Isadora believed in the existence of the pagan deities, and that she accepted all the events of her life as being governed by their whim and will.

The Greeks poetically accorded functions and virtues to their Muses, the daughters of Zeus and Mnemosyne, or Memory. These sisters had power over the arts, Terpsichore ruling over dance. The Hellenic mode in Rhythmic Movement drew together dance, music, poetry and drama, with no separation between, born of a single human instinct toward rhythm.

In invoking the Muses, Isadora Duncan was fancifully

translating her own articulate and masterful grasp of a new dance, a dance which would rely not on aerial acrobatics for physical spectacle and on trivial musical accompaniment for aural stimulation, but on the conjoined powers of rhythm and poetic feeling.

She was far in advance of her time in the boldness of her vision. In an age when women's legs were referred to as "limbs," and prudery had developed frilled chintz petticoats for piano legs, lest these walnut or mahogany appendages arouse impure thoughts, Isadora Duncan believed in the sacredness of the nude human body. She was to dare to write, when she was famous enough to make others listen to what she chose to say, that only the movements of the naked body can be perfectly beautiful. "The noblest art is the nude. This truth is recognized by all, and followed by painters, sculptors, and poets. Only the dancer has forgotten it, who should remember it, as the instrument of [the dance] art is the human body itself."

Utterly sincere, Isadora scandalized all but the most advanced audiences. To a great number of Americans she was to remain a half-naked woman disporting herself immodestly onstage. When she appeared in a recital of *Omar Khayyam*, dancing to the reading of a popular speaker, ladies rose and left the concert hall declaring that they had been offended by the sight of a woman dancing in a state of virtual nudity. She had discarded corsets. Isadora was not well received back in Chicago, her charming natural dances having now become too personal in expression to suit the mass. Opinion hardened and set in America that Isadora Duncan was an immoral woman because she danced immorally. Yet there was nothing suggestively lewd in her dance.

Isadora never doubted her ability to carry her message of Beauty to the world. When she seemed to be halted in reaching her goals she waited for one of the "signs" by which she believed her life was ruled through the gods. Throughout her life she described her most unpredictable actions as having been designed and ordered, and revealed to her in secret. She confided in friends that from childhood she had had visions which other, more sensible people would call hallucinations. She accepted them as portents of her destiny. To the friends who loved her Isadora was a phenomenon, a law to herself and to all who believed in her.

Born under the zodiac sign of Gemini, the Twins, she believed she possessed an alter ego, or other self, and that fire and water were elements closely involved with her destiny. On St. Patrick's Day, 1899, the Hotel Windsor in New York, where the Duncans were staying, burned. The Duncan family lost everything, including Isadora's costumes. But their lives — and those of President Mc-Kinley's family, who were also guests at the hotel — were saved. Isadora had twice been saved from fire, in San Francisco as an infant, and in New York as a woman. She took this as her "sign" that she must turn to water in search of her goal. The broad expanse of the Atlantic Ocean was water enough.

The Duncans tried to raise funds by giving recitals, the mother playing the piano, the boys reading poetry and reciting dramatic speeches and the girls, chiefly Isadora, dancing. The financial gains were meager, not because the Duncans were below the current standard of entertainers, but because the New York newspapers ridiculed them mercilessly, helping to form popular opinion about their worth. Isadora was reduced to begging from her rich patrons, for whom she had danced at soirées, for enough money to pay her and her mother's boat fares to England. Some of these New York patrons gave her introductions to London society and these letters were to prove more useful than bank notes. In London Isadora and her mother at first slept on park benches and ate the cheapest food they could buy, including tomatoes. At that time, tomatoes were suspected of being poisonous and were called "love apples" in the belief that it was a tomato which Eve made Adam eat in the Garden of Eden. In later years, when Isadora was asked how she had fared on arriving in Europe, she replied dramatically: "I was nourished on the Apples of Love!"

The beautiful young American girl was soon taken up by society in London, where art patrons interested themselves in her work. Most profitably for Isadora, she came under the influence of a group of wealthy Englishmen who called themselves "the Hellenics," and were pledged to a Grecian Renaissance. Writers and painters had largely set the vogue for antique Greek forms, their inspiration being the archaeological excavations in Greek lands.

These discoveries influenced every art from architecture through literature and sculpture, and London was so enthused over Greek thought that fashion adopted a taste for the Grecian mode. Hostesses "did over" their drawing rooms and reigning beauties wore gowns and coiffures in the Greek style. England's most popular painter, Sir Lawrence Alma-Tadema, was famous for his portraits on themes from Greek and Greco-Roman life. His paintings were not only hung in the Royal Academy and in magnificent private galleries but were reproduced in cheap lithographs and sold to the public in shops.

This English idyll of the Periclean Age absorbed Isadora Duncan and at once bewitched her.

She made friends of considerable influence and often danced for guests at Alma-Tadema's studio. He took the little American on a tour of museums and led her toward a study of ancient Greek vases, and so into her work from this source. Isadora became the friend of a distinguished Hellenic scholar and historian, Jane Harrison, and of an eminent musicologist, John Fuller-Maitland. The first widened Isadora's knowledge of her beloved Greeks, and the second gave her advice that she benefited by. He told her to dance to the music of great masters rather than to the banal compositions usual at that time for dance accompaniment.

Through another good friend, Sir Charles Hallé, Isadora was presented to royalty. "Evenings with Isadora Duncan" were under the patronage of H. R. H. the Princess of Schleswig-Holstein, Queen Victoria's daughter.

Once Isadora had danced in cheap muslin, dyed and sewn by Mrs. Duncan. Now she wore Liberty silk and, sponsored by a princess, performed for audiences made up of the intellectual and artistic personages of the day. The "half-naked dancer" Duncan had been treated with scant respect in New York, especially by journalists, but in London she numbered among her admirers Sir William Richmond, a painter of the Royal Academy, and Arnold Dolmetsch, a musicologist and expert on antique art.

Isadora succeeded not by her beauty and youth alone but because she convinced these important and eminent persons of the integrity of her dance. She belonged to an era of great beauties among whom she might have passed unnoticed. In London there were as many lithographs sold of society beauties as of actresses, singers and dancers. Some were American heiresses and famous belles. But Isadora was unique among all these because she had the power to describe and express in movement as poets did in words and composers in music.

And Isadora continued to upset traditions and shock the conventional. Now she did so through her use of music. In the philosopher Nietzsche's concept of music there was a division between music in which the spirit dances and music in which the spirit swims; or, music as an art with two separate natures, one useful to the street and theatre, and the other a purely transcendental thing. The popular opinions governing the use of music, in Isadora's time, were drawn from Nietzschean ideas. The dance was generally accompanied by music that was functional, a vehicle, as it were, for the dancer. Even when music was especially composed as accompaniment for dance it was held within the Nietzschean ideal, so that Isadora's use of Beethoven's Seventh Symphony as music for one of her dances caused a furor. The pedantic felt that she was trespassing beyond the bounds allowed the dancer by making use of music which had been composed not as dance accompaniment but as a symphonic form, pure music in itself and therefore too lofty and spiritual for the dancer's purpose. Isadora, however, felt that through dance she was transcribing a visual power as great as the composer's music. Here was begun the danced visualization or interpretation of great musical compositions which would give the twentieth-century dance a new poetic dimension.

Isadora's friends took her to the great art galleries and museums of the European continent and she delightedly exclaimed that here were the treasures of civilization, waiting for her to discover and use for the dance! She became the personification of one great painting, Botticelli's *La Primavera*. Many thought her the veritable incarnation of Woman and Beauty, an idealized human being, Springtime.[18] A contemporary said that the costume which Isadora copied from the central figure of Botticelli's painting looked like a torn rag when it was hanging on a peg in the dancer's dressing room but became "the raiment of Venus" when Isadora put it on and danced.

With fashionable London at her feet and coteries of

rich and influential friends, Isadora now set her heart on conquering Paris. She went there in 1900, during the Exposition Universelle. The year, she said, was appropriate for her invasion of the European theatre because she was a prophet of the new century. And, indeed, it was in Paris, the stronghold and cradle of seventeenth-century ballet, that Isadora found her true home. Here she was accepted as a serious artist, unqualified by her behavior as a woman. In America, Isadora's love affairs would forever (even beyond her death) cause more comment than her dancing.

Isadora expounded her ideas to respectful listeners. She described herself as the Priestess of Dance, and dance as the great freedom which would liberate society from false values and sickly sentimentality. She would oust all that was sham and replace it with dazzling truth, truth strong and pure enough to exist of itself. And, to Isadora, all that was natural, all that was "of Nature," was true.

There were huge gaps in her knowledge. Remembering from her California days the precepts of the teacher Delsarte, she begged to be taken to the great man so that she might kneel at his feet, and learned that he had died before she was born. Some of her statements were profound enough to compel the attention of educated men, but many were childish. Isadora remained superb in her self-confidence. This was her armor and her weapon against all who ridiculed her.

It is true that her poetic ideas about dance were not concisely expressed, but she could be surprisingly precise about certain aspects of her dance, and she very clearly stated her inspiration from Greek art. Inaccurately, she is said to have copied the positions of figures on ancient Grecian vases. What she did, and explained herself as doing, was to find a synthesis of the sequences of natural movement; "of the laws of nature, wherein all is the expression of unending, ever-increasing evolution, wherein are no ends and no beginnings." The thesis here is that of Greek religious thought; of immortality through cycles of successive decline and death (winter) and rebirth (spring), which defy oblivion.

Isadora thought of herself as pure Greek, akin to the Greeks in body and spirit, but she never imitated the static figures of Greek art. She stated: "I . . . take examples of each pose and gesture in the thousands of figures we have left to us in the Greek vases and bas-reliefs; there is not one which in its movements does not presuppose another movement. . . . Dancing naked upon the earth I naturally fall into Greek positions, for Greek positions are only earth positions."

This statement has been misconstrued to mean that Isadora danced in the nude. She never appeared nude in a theatre performance, and her meaning of "dancing naked upon the earth" was that she was moving in close harmony and natural rhythm with the earth. She had divested herself of corsets and petticoats, and often danced in bare feet and with unbound hair. These alterations from the costume of women in ballet and on the street were sufficient to label her "naked" in her contemporary society. It is more than likely that Isadora's costumes would seem almost saintly in our era.

Although Isadora Duncan was a beautiful and graceful woman she was never guilty of self-love and the intent to display her body for coquetry. In fact, she took so detached a view of her body that she referred to it as her "instrument" in an effort to make its function for dance understood. It was the sacredness of the human body, the physical image of the Self, which Isadora preached as her doctrine of beauty. She never once advocated admiration for Isadora Duncan, and she hoped that her personality as a woman would be lost in the impersonality and the elemental nature of Dance. She wished her audiences to see her body become an abstract conception of Rhythmic Life.

When she explained that she was not dancing antique or primitive or "Greek dance," she stressed that it was the Greek ideal of dance which inspired her; dance as a high religious art. "For art which is not religious is not art," wrote Isadora. "It is mere merchandise."

But in the puritanical American society from which she had come, her critics persisted in labeling her a "barefoot" dancer and other derogatory names. Few at home understood that her so-called nudity was from the purest artistic requirements that her body or "instrument" be free to express its design in dance. Her aims were clearly stated and in terms practical for the dancer today: "The dancer [is] one whose body and soul have grown so harmoniously together that the natural language of that soul will have become the movement of the body . . . From all parts of her body shall shine radiant intelligence . . ."

The "intelligence" of which Duncan spoke was not that of the "intellectual" or "cerebral" dance styles which followed hers. Rather, Duncan meant this kind of intelligence: "There are those who, subconsciously, hear with their souls some melody of another world, and are able to express this in terms comprehensible and joyous to human ears. . . . Imagine then a dancer who, after long study, prayer and inspiration, has attained such a degree of understanding that his body is simply the luminous manifestation of his soul; whose body dances in accordance with the music heard inwardly, in an expression out of another, a profounder world. This is the truly creative dancer, natural but not imitative, speaking in movement out of himself and out of something greater than ourselves."

Isadora saw that she must teach her precepts to students of dance, or these precepts would perish when she ceased dancing. She had a passion to teach, which was shared by no other pioneers of Modern Dance except Shawn and Humphrey. In the main, the Modern dancers were chiefly concerned with personal statements in dance. But Isadora realized that her ideal of dance was so unconventional to the era that she must convey it to fresh young bodies and minds, to students innocent of false values, without prejudices and prides or self-consciousness. She chose twenty girls aged four to eight years, and not only taught them to dance but reared them according to her ideas of what were, for the human dancer, "most moral, healthful and beautiful." Six of these children she eventually adopted as her wards and they assumed the name "Duncan." One of them, Irma, who worked with Duncan until Duncan's death, wrote *The Technique of Isadora Duncan*. A text on Duncanesque dance, it includes the dance based on the Tanagra figurines.[19]

This little book is illustrated with photographs of Isadora, Irma and other Duncan pupils. It brings to our eyes today as close and clear a view as may be visually seized of Duncan's fabled dancing. Pictures of her are, to our eyes, as illustrative and as maddeningly illusive as the Tanagra figurines were to Isadora, for they only show single arrested poses from movements of once living dancers. They do not re-create Isadora and her dance, for these lived and were animate and eloquent through the now-vanished spirit, as well as the forms.

The "natural" and "rhythmic movement" which Isadora recognized and used in her dance survive, and were incorporated in the works of her successors, but her dance was so personal and its beauty was so inherent to Duncan that not even her protégées could re-create it.

She left no real choreographic text for dance, and the relationship which ideally exists between the ballet teacher and student, or choreographer and dancer, was not so marked for Isadora and her pupils. Her rapport, the close awareness of her dance, was with her audiences, and it is from memories recorded by her contemporaries that we best recapture the image of Isadora's dancing. For all her insistence, the dancer's identity could not be kept free of the woman's — perhaps because Isadora lived as she danced, a free soul, flouting conventions.

These conventions were far stricter than in our time, and Isadora appeared far more outrageous to her society than she would to ours. She had liaisons with men and bore illegitimate children and her critics damned her "free dance" as part and parcel of her cult of "free love." A writer called her "the female Byron; mad, bad and dangerous to know." Respectable young ladies were forbidden to attend her performances. It became voguish for young men to fall madly in love with the "Venus of Dance." Isadora, who called herself Aphrodite, was now named "the love-goddess," the synonym for seductive beauty and amorous notoriety later applied to movie stars — Rita Hayworth in the 1940s, Ingrid Bergman in the 1950s, and Elizabeth Taylor in the 1960s.

In Budapest she had an affair with an actor, Oscar Beregi, whom she named "Romeo" after first seeing him in Shakespeare's play. Marriage to Beregi was against her feminist "pact" not to subjugate herself to a man; besides, the Hungarian expected her to give up dancing and settle down in Budapest as a housewife.

Isadora's intuition that her fortune lay abroad was correct, for her instantaneous success in Europe brought her the admiration and friendship of famous people. On her arrival in Paris her friend Hallé introduced her not only to the treasures of the Louvre but also to influential Parisians. When Isadora made her Paris debut in dance no less a personage than Maurice Ravel was her pianist. Isadora was launched by her fellow-American Fuller, who was herself an intimate of royal and diplomatic society. In February 1902 Fuller presented Isadora Duncan to a fashionable audience in Vienna. Duncan appeared in gauze drapery which barely concealed nudity, causing Fuller a momentary qualm. But the intellectuals applauded the new American dancer, and an impresario, Alexander Grosz, arranged a triumphal European tour for Isadora.

It was on this tour that she met Beregi, whom she then put out of her mind very quickly. On the invitation of Frau Wagner, she danced at the Wagnerian Festival in Bayreuth. For the first time, she danced within a group, as the leading Grace in the *Tannhäuser* Bacchanal.

Isadora was now twenty-six, her genius recognized, her position without peer in the theatre. The German people were especially worshipful, and she founded a school, in 1904, at Grünewald, near Berlin. It was here that she installed her first pupils, with her Duncan relatives in charge during her absence. Famous people who had once been names without reality were now her friends, among them the English actress Ellen Terry. And Isadora met and fell in love with Terry's son, Gordon Craig.

Craig was a revolutionary influence in theatre, an artist-designer whose disgust with the era's theatre style provoked him into ideas for reforming it. Many of his ideas were put into effect, and he, as well as Fuller, influenced the English and European stage to a considerable extent. The basis of Craig's ideas was the return to a more serious and profound development and coordination of the arts of the theatre. His principles were such that Isadora felt an affinity for him as a fellow-artist, but she saw him as bound to his work as she was to hers. She would not marry Craig, but she lived with him, believing that their work and their love were so strong and important that they needed no other bonds.

Of note is the fact that Craig was himself the natural son of Ellen Terry and Edward William Godwin, an architect and theatrical designer of the English theatre. But Miss Terry had lived with Godwin discreetly in retirement from the stage, while Isadora continued to dance through her love affairs and her pregnancies, barely interrupting her work long enough to give birth to her children. She left Craig, without telling him that she was carrying a child, to go to St. Petersburg in 1905. It was her greatest artistic challenge, dancing for audiences accustomed to the splendid Russian Imperial Ballet and its dazzling ballerinas.

Ballet had descended to the music hall level in England and to vaudeville in America, and persons of taste in those countries looked on ballet dancing as puerile. Isadora and her contemporary, the American author Edith Wharton, shared the same opinion of ballet, that it was a meaningless spectacle of pirouettes. The nobility of the ballet had ebbed with the rising popularity for the spectacular at the expense of the aesthetic. This was the prevalent theatrical standard against which Craig rebelled. But while the European ballet deteriorated through the latter part of the nineteenth century, the Russian Imperial Theatres raised the art to its epitome through a combination of excellent teachers, gifted choreographers, and fine dancers. Isadora had been quoted as stating that the ballet was sterile of expression and shackling in technique, and in Russia there were some who agreed with her, among them a young choreographer, Michel Fokine.

A year before Isadora arrived in St. Petersburg Fokine submitted to the directors of the Imperial Theatre his thesis for a new form of ballet, a fusion of dance, music and painting. Fokine's ideas were discouraged by the directors, and the form of the stage ballet remained as of old.

Compared to the sumptuous Russian ballet, Isadora was stunning in her naturalness and simplicity. Instead of tons of mechanical scenery, she danced with only her "Duncan blue" draperies. From Fuller and Craig she had absorbed a great deal of skill about lighting. Her music was borrowed from the masters of that art. In a filmy Greek chiton, her legs and feet bare, her hair loose, Isadore danced to a Chopin étude. The Russians received her in all seriousness, and her "free" style electrified the artists who advocated Fokine's natural principles.

Her influence on Fokine appeared in his ballet *Eunice* in 1907. It was danced in bare feet and Greek tunics. Fokine's Five Principles for the ballet,[20] which established him as "the father of modern ballet," were expressed with more succinctness than Isadora's romantic descriptions of her dance, but between these two revolutionaries of twentieth-century dancing there was mutual emphasis on naturalness and truth. Fokine reformed twentieth-century ballet without destroying its technique, and the ballet maintained its awesome discipline of training for the student, whereas Isadora advocated freedom for the body through the impulse of the spirit. She and Fokine may be said to have been in sympathy if not in perfect accord, and after Fokine and Duncan the ballet assumed a more human element, with a naturalness and eloquence of gesture different from the stylized form of the nineteenth-century dance.

From St. Petersburg, Isadora traveled to Moscow, where Constantin Stanislavsky, the genius of the Moscow Art Theatre, became her great admirer, as he relates in his autobiography *My Life in Art*.[21] Stanislavsky's methods would later shake the American stage, methods which had received the magnetic influence of the American dancer, Duncan.

She had not confided the secret of her pregnancy to anyone, not even her mother and sister, and now Isadora stole away alone to a little village near Leyden, Holland, to bear her child. She who was usually the "joyous dancer" became prey to forebodings that she would die in childbirth and that no one would care for her child. She was never free of the fear of death by violent means, either through fire or water. To add to her fear of fire, from which she had twice narrowly escaped, she feared water ever since 1898, when her father, his third wife and their child died in a shipwreck. Fascinated by her fears, she chose to await the birth of her child near the sea. While she waited she tried to compose new dances for teaching her pupils which would give them insight into dance but would leave them free to dance from impulse alone.[22]

She dreamed one night that Ellen Terry came to her, leading by the hand a glorious infant who was Gordon Craig's child. In panic, Isadora sent for an old friend, a Scottish sculptress named Kathleen Bruce. Miss Bruce awoke one night and found Isadora's bed empty. Rushing down to the beach she saw her friend wading far out into the water, and when Miss Bruce brought her back to shore Isadora seemed half asleep, unconscious of danger.

The child was born September 24, 1905, very blonde, exquisitely beautiful. At her father's wish she was named Deirdre, for the heroine of an Irish legend. Isadora believed that the child had been created for a special purpose, and always spoke of her as "Ellen Terry's grandchild."

Radiant, Isadora returned to the stage and to supervising her school in Grünewald, where she had established Elizabeth and Mrs. Duncan. Augustin, discarding the e in his name, had become an actor. Raymond, married to a Greek wife, was dispatched to build a temple of dance on property Isadora had purchased in Greece.

On her third engagement in Russia, where her popularity was now so great that she was hailed as a savant of the dance, Isadora took with her thirteen of her Grünewald pupils. Her personal success was enhanced by this troupe, nicknamed the "Isadorables," but she was dissatisfied with the work at Grünewald, feeling herself hampered by the restrictions of German officialism. She wished to establish schools in England and France and was disappointed that neither country's government offered to found them for her. So now she turned back toward America to test her welcome at home after ten triumphant years in foreign countries.

Her reception was polite enough in Washington, where President Theodore Roosevelt led an audience in applause, but the majority of Americans violently disapproved of the ways in which Isadora danced, and above all, the life that Isadora boldly lived. They saw her as the mother of a child born out of wedlock; it did not matter in the least that this beautiful child was Ellen Terry's granddaughter and the daughter of two important artists in the theatre. The six-month contract made with the impresario Charles Frohman was canceled, and Isadora and Deirdre sailed back to Europe.

In 1909 Isadora had no rival as a dancer, even among the prima ballerinas of the ballet. The Russian impresario Serge Diaghilev launched a renaissance in European ballet by bringing to Paris a troupe from the Russian Imperial Ballet.[23] But not even these great dancers could eclipse Isadora. She continued to dance to adoring audiences. More, these audiences now included many ballet dancers, who came to study Isadora's matchless art.

She had the satisfaction of knowing that Fokine and

other Diaghilev choreographers incorporated into the "modern" ballet some of the precepts she had inaugurated for her "new" dance of the twentieth century.

The freedom that Isadora advocated for the dancer, which extended from physical technique to costuming, resulted in the plasticity and expressiveness now ordinary to both ballet and Modern Dance. Isadora decreed that the whole body, the whole being, must dance. The revolutionary idea stretched far beyond the stage and the costume of the dancer. It was observed in the street dress of women of fashion, and (according to some psychologists and sociologists) affected the emancipation of women in business, politics and social work, and especially in matters of feminine beauty and hygiene.

Isadora now spoke as a pedagogue, and writers wrote eulogies in her honor. In the theatre, famous painters sketched her and intellectuals like Edith Wharton commented, with awe, on the immense, rapt audiences who came to watch Isadora dance. In an engagement at the Théâtre Gaîté-Lyrique in Paris, Isadora presided like an empress in the Green Room after performances. Parisian society, and every visitor to Paris of consequence in commerce, politics or art, paid court to Isadora. Here came the man she named "Lohengrin" after Wagner's hero, to join the throng of Isadora's masculine admirers.

"Lohengrin" was Paris Eugene Singer, the twenty-second child of Isaac Singer, the sewing machine millionaire. He was as handsome, gallant and romantic as a fairy-tale prince. Besides being exceedingly rich, Singer was socially well connected, his sister having married into an aristocratic European family. He was an intimate of the King and Queen of England and owned a yacht, the *Isis*, on which he proposed to steal away with Isadora. Their cosmopolitan friends thought it a perfect romance and Isadora the obvious "Helen" for this modern Paris.

There was one impediment to this beautiful romance, and that was the fact that Paris was married and the father of five children. His wife refused to divorce him, but Singer and Isadora sailed on the *Isis* to his villa on the French Riviera.

Between her theatre engagements, Isadora lived openly with Singer in his Paris house in the Place des Vosges and on an estate he owned in England. In 1910 Singer took her to Egypt. They sailed the Nile in a *dahabeah*, a native boat, and Isadora declared that here she was as near to Paradise as she would ever be. She was Cleopatra and Helen, Aphrodite and Isis, every woman and goddess fabled for love and beauty. Singer surrounded her and her daughter with every luxury and hired the architect Louis Sue to design and build her a theatre in Paris. The plan for the theatre did not materialize, because Isadora wanted to set it on the Champs Elysées and the French Government would not permit it.

She made another visit to the United States and met with the same reception as before; cautious admiration from a few, violent criticism from the mass. She bore a son, Patrick, to Singer in 1911.

The two ensuing years were the happiest in Isadora's

life. In the spring of 1913 there was not another woman who had so much. She and her two children were so beautiful that people stopped to watch them pass on the street. Isadora loved her children with the headlong passion and energy she brought to life. They were blond and blue-eyed and she called them her angels. Isadora herself was the most talked-about, written-about, painted and sculptured woman alive. Her German school was thriving and Singer had promised her his help to found other schools in England and France. As a dancer she was without peer, and her beauty, at thirty-five, seemed indestructible. She had a lovely oval face, long lustrous hair and a body which was like no other woman's.

On April 19, Isadora kissed her children as they got into Singer's limousine with their nurse. They were going for a ride to Versailles. The sun was shining, the Seine sparkled, and Deirdre and Patrick waved to their mother through the car window.

A little way off the automobile stalled and the chauffeur got out to crank it. He forgot to put on the brake, and the car slid backward into the river. The two children and their nurse were drowned.

Isadora behaved like a madwoman. She cut off her hair and threw it into the sea as Isis had done. When it grew out again it was white. Raymond Duncan and his Greek wife Penelope were on an expedition to Epirus to aid the survivors of the recent Turkish-Balkan war, and Isadora went to them, hoping that the sorrows of strangers would teach her how to bear her own.

With the outbreak of World War I the German school was evacuated to England and thence to America. Elizabeth and Augustin went with the pupils and the impresario Sol Hurok arranged a tour for Isadora. She danced at the Metropolitan Opera House in New York for a great audience, realizing a triumph she had long coveted. Here, where she had been ridiculed and condemned, she received homage for her dancing. The little "Irisher" of the wretched California days had come a long way and by a thorny path to the apex of her national theatre.

With the loss of her children she was more intent than ever on devoting herself to dance, and she believed she could use its power for peace. In 1921 she returned to Russia, thinking that the Revolution had destroyed the Imperial Ballet and that the people would eagerly adopt her free, new dance. She had a vision of "a thousand happy children dancing to a symphony," by which she would create "a wave of brotherhood" to drown hatred and unite Europe and Russia.

In Russia Isadora met the poet Serge Esenin. He was twenty-seven; she was forty-three. That April, the anniversary of her children's drowning, her mother died. Singer was paralyzed by a stroke. Isadora was lonely and alone. What reason had she for living, except to bring joy to someone? This was her explanation for marrying Esenin and taking him to America. The Russian poet was an epileptic and an alcoholic, too ill to be cured by Isadora's well-meant but inept kindness. In America he got blood poisoning from drinking Prohibition alcohol. Violent and morose by turns, Esenin became increasingly difficult to control, and Isadora took him to Paris where, on the advice of physicians, she placed him in a private sanitarium.

Her luck had deserted her. She who once could do no wrong now could do no right. Although she maintained Esenin in a private hospital at great expense, the Russian expatriates in Paris attacked her for confining the poet in a madhouse. Meanwhile, in America, the evangelist Billy Sunday was denouncing her from the pulpit as a "scarlet woman," and her fellow-Americans indignantly called her a bolshevist and Soviet-sympathizer because she wished to establish a school in Russia. No one had offered to help her found a school in the United States, and she accepted the Soviets' establishment of a Duncan school of dance. When Isadora returned to Russia with Esenin, he committed suicide. Isadora left the school in her pupil Irma Duncan's charge and went back to Paris.

She had been a joyous dancer, *La Primavera*, of whom Caroline and Charles Caffin, contemporary writers, said in 1912: "For sheer beauty and gladness . . . that brings happy tears to the eyes and catches the breath in a sob in the throat, few things in life equal one's first experience of the dancing of Isadora Duncan." But the deaths of her children killed the joy of *La Primavera*. No longer the manifestation of a glorious Springtime, Isadora began her work as a tragedienne, composing patriotic pieces of dance like *Marche Slave* and *La Marseillaise*. The somber but exalted works touched audiences who had lately known the grief and horror of the war, and Isadora's genius was hailed anew and more devotedly than before. Ellen Terry said that she had not seen tragedy until Duncan's *Marche Slave*.

In her personal life, Isadora was bitterly unhappy and lonely. She had disastrous and sordid love affairs in the hope that she would bear children to replace the two she had lost. A pregnancy resulted in a stillborn child, and Isadora believed that she was under a curse. Her great success, in 1927, in the *Tannhaüser* Bacchanal and *Love-Death of Isolde* was marred by litigation over the use of Wagner's music as accompaniment for these dance works.

That summer, nearing her fiftieth birthday, and no longer the lovely young Faun who had traveled so far from her native California, Isadora went to dine with friends at Nice. When the hosts brought their children in to say goodnight, Isadora sprang up and rushed into the street, weeping that she could not bear to live in a world where there were still beautiful, blue-eyed children.

On September 14 she went for a ride with a new acquaintance, a young Italian motorist whose Bugatti sports car she had admired. When he called for her at her hotel Isadora wrapped herself in a long, fringed shawl, throwing one end over her shoulder. As the car started a friend called out that the shawl was trailing on the ground. The car stopped, but Isadora sat still, her face fallen on her breast. The trailing end of the shawl had become entangled in the Bugatti's rear wheel and the tension on the cloth had broken the dancer's neck.

Isadora Duncan died with her work undone, not knowing if the "new" dance would live after her. Her dream of Duncan schools of dance in every country of the world was never realized. The Russian school founded under the Soviets lasted for only a few years. After Duncan's death, Irma Duncan continued in charge for two years and then brought a troupe from the Soviet school to perform in the West. It was recalled by the Soviet Government in 1929 and Irma Duncan Rogers settled in New York to teach in a school she established as "Isadora Duncan Dance Art."

The Duncanesque dance was taught in schools established in Berlin in 1904, Paris in 1914, and Moscow in 1921, and by Irma Duncan and Maria-Theresa Duncan (another of Isadora's six protégées), who headed a group called the Heliconodes. Maria-Theresa was actively performing in spring, 1964, at the Ligoa Duncan Arts Center, New York. No Duncan pupil attained anywhere near the measure of Isadora's renown. Despite the radical changes in Modern Dance, whose forms and spirit today would be alien to Duncan, her ideas and some of her techniques are still currently taught. One Duncanesque teacher is Kathleen Hinni in New York, a pupil of Anita Zahn, who was trained by Irma Duncan.

The styles of Duncanesque dance are labeled with terms such as "interpretive," "Grecian," and "plastique."

Simple verities of movement (walk, run, hop, skip, leap) predicated by graceful deportment was for a long time known as Duncan's way of dancing. Its practitioners had not read Duncan's command: "Don't be merely graceful. Nobody is interested in a lot of graceful young girls. Unless your dancing springs from an inner emotion and expresses an idea, it will be meaningless and the audience will be bored." Nevertheless, long after Isadora, Americans persisted in "Modern Dance" according to the weakest versions of Duncan's precepts, and sometimes in distortion of these.

Duncan's precepts were romantic, for her dance idealized the dancer. She was lyrical in physical expression and artistic interpretation.

In classifying dancers a personal style is always derived as much from the physical and temperamental endowments of the dancer as from the mode in which she dances. Duncan was romantic and lyrical, as was her successor, Ruth St. Denis, and the ideal of feminine beauty passed through them into the early Modern Dance. This must be known and remembered before encountering the influences of other and different dancers such as Graham.

Many dance authorities see the clearest evidence of a Duncan influence within the style of the Moscow Bolshoi Ballet, in the pliancy of the feminine dancers and especially in the rapture of spirit and lyricism of technique with which the Russian dancers perform bacchante roles.

Despite Duncan's influences on the Russians, there is no Modern Dance in Soviet Russia.

In 1957 Irma Duncan Rogers donated her Duncan collection to the New York Public Library. It is in such memorabilia, and a wealth of anecdote and reminiscence, that Isadora Duncan's life and work are preserved.[24]

Denishawn: The Fertile Ground

"DENISHAWN" is a contraction of the names of St. Denis and Shawn, two important pioneers in the American dance theatre. They were dance partners in a company and cofounders of an academy, both of which bore the name Denishawn.

Ruth St. Denis and Ted Shawn married in 1914 and were closely associated in their professional careers until Denishawn was disbanded, some sixteen years after its founding in 1915. Thereafter they separated but were never divorced.

The contraction of their last names into "Denishawn" came about during a tour, when a theatre manager in Portland, Oregon, offered eight box seats to the person submitting the most suitable name for a new and supposedly untitled dance that the company had been programming as *The St. Denis Mazurka*. Mrs. Margaret Ayer of Portland offered the winning name: *The Denishawn Rose Mazurka*, incorporating the dancers' names as one and complimenting Portland, "the City of Roses." Taken by the attractive contraction of their names, Ruth

St. Denis and Ted Shawn thereafter adopted "Denishawn" as the official title of their company.

Denishawn School was first established in Los Angeles, adjacent to Hollywood moving picture studios from which came bevies of stars to study dance. Among these were Mabel Normand, Blanche Sweet, Ruth Chatterton, Lenore Ulric, Roszika and Jeanne — "the Dolly Sisters," Lillian Gish, Ina Claire, Claire Niles, and Barbara and Joan Bennett. But Denishawn was far more than a dancing school. It was actually the fertile ground and stimulating climate for Modern Dance's growth and development in America. It lived up to the purposes for which Shawn planned it: "We stressed the individual in all our teaching, in the dances we choreographed . . . The last thing we wanted to produce was a facsimile row of pupils who would be robot imitators of St. Denis and Shawn. Our role as we saw it was to provide the stimulus, knowledge and experience essential to the development of dance artists, and to give encouragement to the imaginative performer."

To understand how revolutionary were these concepts for the dancer in America we must retrace American dance history to the eras in which St. Denis and Shawn were born and grew up and began to dance. The theatre they helped to make is the theatre which succeeding American dancers inherited, and St. Denis and Shawn, and Denishawn, mark the end of an epoch and the beginning of another in the traditions of our national dance.

✍ Ruth St. Denis

While the fourteen-year-old Dora Duncan was teaching San Franciscans to dance the polka, a twelve-year-old New Jersey girl was climbing into a tree house to munch apples and read Kant's *Critique of Pure Reason*. "Ruthie" Dennis lived on a farm, Pin Oaks, with a younger brother, "Buzz," and their parents; attended village school and a ladies' seminary ruled by Dwight L. Moody; and, for recreation, read every book she could lay hand to.

With a father who was an atheist and electrical engineer, and a mother who was religious and gave lectures on hygiene and aesthetics, Ruth Dennis's literature in childhood ranged from the works of Kant, Tom Paine and Robert Ingersoll to the Bible and Dumas's *Lady of the Camellias*. Her impressionable mind was nurtured on a combination of argumentative (then called "anti-Christian") thought and romance, metaphysics and religion.

Her first dramatic interpretation was of the Crucifixion, at eleven years of age, when she imitated the martyred Jesus. And in reading one book, *The Idyll of the White Lotus* by Mabel Collins, she found her inspiration as a dancer. The Collins book about a young Egyptian priest who had a symbolic vision of the Lady of the White Lotus was to have the most lasting and direct influence on St. Denis. By accident, the New Jersey farm girl was turned toward the East for her dancer's destiny, just as Dora Duncan had been turned toward Athenian Greece.

It is of interest that these two American women were born and reared on opposite sides of their continent and that the Westerner, Duncan, geographically closer to Eastern culture, was the one to set her ideal on the ancient Greeks, while the Easterner, St. Denis, was bewitched by Indo-Asian thought and art.

In one of the best autobiographies ever written by a dancer, St. Denis describes her childhood and the early part of her career as a dancer.[25] Her father was a Civil War veteran, an inventor who dreamed of flying machines while people were debating whether the new fad, the automobile, would last. Her mother was a practicing doctor of medicine before her marriage to T. L. Dennis. Ruth adored her incompatible parents.

Mrs. Dennis was far in advance of her times in ideas of hygiene and feminine independence. She refused to wear corsets and she advocated for her children a way of life in which the Bible and harmonic gymnastics had equal values. Mrs. Dennis studied Delsartian rhythms under Mme Poté, a pupil of Steele MacKaye. Fearing that her tall, tomboy daughter would grow up without graceful deportment, she insisted that Ruth practice exercises from a "grammar" of Delsarte. Every evening after supper the mother sat down in her apron, grammar in hand, and called out instructions to Ruth who, in a petticoat, holding to the rail of her bed, obediently performed contortions called "harmonic gymnastics." In all innocence, the training of the great St. Denis had begun.

Mrs. Dennis loved playacting and produced an entertainment to raise money for a schoolhouse flag. Ruth Dennis, in white cheesecloth, was billed as the curtain raiser in a movement à la Delsarte. The program grossed twenty-five dollars for the flag.

The Dennises were poor and Ruth wore hand-me-down clothing from more prosperous cousins, but she was allowed considerably more freedom than many girls of her time. She enjoyed hours of solitude when she dreamed in her tree house or sat in a swing, rising and falling in a swooping rhythm like flying. Movement exhilarated her.

She was sent to the local dancing school, where her teacher urged Mrs. Dennis to take Ruth to New York to a celebrated teacher named Carl Marwig, a stately old gentleman who dressed for his classes in satin knee-breeches. Ruth picked watercress from the Pin Oaks brook and sold it in the town, Somerville, to earn railroad fares for herself and her mother. Marwig was so impressed by Ruth's talent for dancing that he offered to give her lessons free of charge, but the Dennises could not afford the cost of commuting regularly between New Jersey and New York. Ruth studied intermittently with Marwig whenever there were sufficient funds, and profited by the lessons.

Ruth Dennis improvised dance, but thought of it as

running, leaping, turning, falling down. She was a tall, lanky girl who reached her woman's height before adolescence. Awkward in the parlor at her mother's tea parties, she was strong, sure and secure when she danced in class or skimmed the earth whose rhythms she sensed.

Friends took her to New York, where she saw the Barnum and Bailey circus's *Burning of Rome*, a colossal spectacle whose finale was danced by a hundred "angels" dressed in fluttering ribbons. Returning home, Ruth Dennis rushed up to the attic, cut some old curtains into strips, and improvised an angel dance. Next she was taken to a performance of *Egypt Through The Ages*, another spectacular choreographed and staged by the Kiralfy family, Hungarian dancers who produced a great deal of the American ballet of that era. Dramatic inspiration thus entered Ruth Dennis's imagination to impel her instincts for dance.

Mrs. Dennis took her child to a concert performance by Genevieve Stebbins, who made an ineradicable impression on the girl. The dancer wore soft white robes and seemed to Ruth Dennis to gleam like a pearl against the green draperies that she used — as Duncan's dance was to feature her own shade of blue. Mrs. Stebbins danced as Niobe and Terpsichore and the incarnations of "the Hours of the Day." She convinced Ruth Dennis that the dance could express the beauty and dignity of the human being.

At sixteen and largely self-taught, Ruth went with her mother to New York and got her first job at a vaudeville theatre, Worth's, on Thirtieth Street. It was a type of theatre prevalent in that era, offering vaudeville acts and museum exhibits. Ruth Dennis earned twenty dollars a week dancing eleven times a day a single number called *Gavotte d'Amour.*

It was not the sixteenth-century gavotte and had no concern with love. It consisted, as a "dance piece," of backbends, cartwheels, splits, and the "slow kick." This last was a feat greatly admired by the era's audiences, being gymnastics in which the performer brought her right leg up to touch the sole of its foot to the forehead, and then reversed the movement with the left leg, laying the sole of that foot at the back of the head. When such contortions were executed slowly and in some sort of rhythmic harmony with a musical "accompaniment" it was considered "dance." If the executant wore the traditional pink ballet shoes then this sort of dancing was "ballet."

The dancer of this time was hired and advertised as "a Terpsichorean artiste of fantastic grace and agility" to "insert feats of dance activity" into "colossal spectacles." To audiences of the day, dancers were "high kickers" and "toe twirlers," and they were reputed, willy-nilly, to be frivolous young women. A large percentage of that audience seriously believed that the "little bally dancer" spent her spare time quaffing champagne from her dancing slippers.[26]

Born in 1880, St. Denis began her dancing career in the era dominated by theatrical performers like "Little

Egypt," the famous hootchy-kootchy dancer whose "art" was so valued that the producers of her act insured her for $25,000 against hip dislocation. Entering the theatre in 1896, St. Denis was within the decade of the Gay Nineties. It was not only a decade but a phase in American culture, with a style strongly influenced by Lillian Russell, the beloved of Diamond Jim Brady. Dance was exceedingly popular, if extremely suspect as being immoral, and a dancer named Frankie Bailey became a household synonym for "legs" because hers were considered the epitome of beauty and dexterity.

Ruth Dennis and some others were determined to win fame in their theatre but longed to perform aesthetically. "Aesthetic" dance was much the vogue, and some concert dance was performed in modes "Delsartian," "Neo-Grecian," and "plastique" as "harmonic gymnastics and aesthetics," to separate them, definitely, from the more popular mode of dance which blatantly advertised "legs, legs, legs, and more legs!" [27]

Ruth Dennis was well received by the audiences of Worth's theatre but regularly flung herself, weeping, into her mother's arms when she reached the wings after an ovation for *Gavotte d'Amour*. She wished to dance in the Stebbins style, while theatrical promoters and the mass audience in America wanted dancing à la Frankie Bailey. Mrs. Dennis wryly remarked on this as she dried Ruth's tears.

While attending high school Ruth Dennis filled engagements for which she was hired by a New York agent, and became popular with gentlemen's clubs in much the way that Duncan scored her early triumphs with the Press Club in San Francisco and "Old Bohemia" in Chicago. But while Isadora Duncan had towed her mother in her train, Mrs. Dennis was a dragon of a chaperone, as much intent on the preservation of her daughter's good reputation as the pursuit of a career.

Ruth Dennis was a lovely girl with long brown hair and the figure and gracefulness fashionable in her day as "willowy." She was mercurial by temperament, and fun-loving. Ruth St. Denis is the wittiest and most naturally mischievous woman ever to grace the annals of Modern Dance. Her natural charm and indolence would in all likelihood have ruined her career except for the indomitable mother who ruled her life until her marriage and thereafter exerted considerable domination until Mrs. Dennis's death. But even when she was hailed as a great and serious artiste in Europe, Ruth St. Denis remained incorrigibly humorous, unaffected by the pomp and circumstance which attended her as the successor of Isadora Duncan.

This position in the Modern Dance came about only after St. Denis went to Europe in 1904. Like Duncan in earlier years of the same era, St. Denis's personal art of dance was not appreciated in the United States until the Europeans established her as a theatrical star.

St. Denis, in the course of her rise to fame, was a vaudeville "ballet girl," depending on some basic studies of the ballet technique and her ability and strength to dance on the tips of her toes. She was a student, very briefly, of the same Bonfanti who taught Duncan. Bonfanti dismissed Dennis as a student after teaching her the first three of the five basic ballet positions, and Dennis's "ballet technique" depended largely on lessons from Marwig and the tenacity with which she copied the dancing of two popular New York "stars of the ballet," Bessie Clayton and Marguerite Clarke.

The Dennis family moved to Brooklyn, and Ruth lost the country life she had loved at Pin Oaks. But she now became a member of the David Belasco company, the star of which was the celebrated Mrs. Leslie Carter. Ruth Dennis was hired for a tiny "ballet girl" role in *Zaza*, one of Mrs. Carter's most popular plays, and nearly lost her job at the first rehearsal because of her irrepressible comic sense and her power of mimicry.

The costumes of the "ballet girls" were not of the freshest, and Ruth commented that the tutus looked like wet hens, they were so tired and bedraggled. Encouraged by her fellow chorines, Miss Dennis staged an impromptu "dance of the wet hen." Mrs. Carter, a formidable creature, was not one of Ruth's admirers and from her unequalled power in the company ordered her fired. Ruth was saved through the intercession of a pitying stage manager, who arranged for a "staged apology" to pacify Mrs. Carter. Faced with the tyrant queen of the American stage, Dennis forgot her lines as rehearsed with the stage manager, struggled not to burst out laughing, and suffered an attack of the hiccoughs to which she was prone. Mrs. Carter misunderstood the hiccoughs for sobs and majestically dismissed the "weeping" chorus girl — who was laughing just as hard as Mrs. Carter believed she was crying.

Belasco, noting the charm and beauty of Miss Dennis, gave her a permanent place in his company and a new title. He removed one *n* from her name and prefixed it with St. to mock and commend her on the moral scruples which made St. Denis a celebrity backstage long before she became famous to the audience.

St. Denis traveled in America and to England with the Belasco company and appeared to settle into a career as an actress. In Buffalo, New York, she found her destiny in a drug store. She stopped there to enjoy a soda with Patsy, her best friend in the company, and was enchanted by a poster, 18 by 24 inches, on the wall behind the soda counter. It advertised a brand of cigarettes, "Egyptian Deities," and depicted the goddess Isis seated on a throne, holding a lotus, with her feet in the waters of the Nile. Here was the "Lady of the Lotus" which had spurred Ruth Dennis's childish imagination at Pin Oaks. The grown-up Ruth St. Denis saw herself in the figure of the woman who symbolized feminine power and beauty to the ancient Egyptians — as did Aphrodite for the ancient Greeks.

St. Denis bought the cigarette poster from the drug store clerk for a dollar and made a costume in imitation of that worn in the picture by Isis. In San Francisco she spent her last five dollars having a Japanese photographer make studies of her in the "Isis pose." As the Belasco company turned homeward from California, St. Denis (with only her loyal roommate, Patsy, in on the secret) planned her own incarnation as Egypta.

Mrs. Dennis, like Patsy, was impressed, but there was no money to mount and stage the dance production Ruth envisioned as *Egypta*. However, she was sure that she would find a stage and an audience after she had invented the dance. Her research ranged from New York museums of Egyptian art to Coney Island exhibits of the popular "hootchy-kootchy" dancers, whose style had become widely admired from "Little Egypt's" sensational debut at the St. Louis Fair. In searching for material for a dance called *Egypta*, St. Denis discovered the *devi-dassi*, the temple dancers of Indian religion, and was entranced with them as potential subjects for dance.

She made friends with Indian emigrés in New York, some of whom were students in colleges, others clerks in Oriental-import shops. She brought them home to Mrs. Dennis in Brooklyn, where the Dennis family to supplement their meager income took in paying guests. Her exotic friends talked to her about India, its religion and dance, and helped her to comprehend these foreign forms, so far removed from the middle-class American Christian culture of the 1890s, by beating native music on their drums. Ruth Dennis drank in the impressions and emotions she received from the Indians, who poured out to her their ardent love for Mother India. Mrs. Dennis was always present, the dragon chaperone, but she was an intelligent and practical help to her daughter and a

genius at organizing the details that Ruth often overlooked in her desire to seize upon the whole of a dance
work.

Mrs. Dennis overruled her husband, who had doubts
about his daughter going into the theatre, by insisting
that if their child's work lay onstage then that was where
Ruth must go in search of it. But she forced Ruth to work
on that stage when Ruth often would have preferred to
play. Mrs. Dennis kept friends from taking up too much
of her daughter's time. When Ruth gathered an audience
for a rehearsal of a work and the rehearsal slipped into a
party, Mrs. Dennis intervened. She cleaned up the kitchen
after the Indian friends had cooked smoking hot curries
for refreshment, and it was Mrs. Dennis who organized, catalogued, and checked and rechecked big and little details, from costumes to theatre schedules. Dryly re-
marking that Ruth had a talent for choosing the right
colors and fabrics but would, as like as not, cut two left
sleeves and none for the right, Mrs. Dennis supervised
the costumes for the dances Ruth composed. Ruth created the first of these, *The Cobras*, in part at the Dennis
breakfast table, with salt and pepper shakers and bits of
toast. As a critic, Mrs. Dennis had a quick, shrewd, un-
erring sense for theatrical effect.[28]

St. Denis used Clément Delibes's *Lakmé* as music for
The Cobras and *Radha*, which she performed for gentlemen's "smokers." Two years passed, and St. Denis appeared in vaudeville and soirées, always more of a fad

than an artist to her audiences. In general, she was treated as a "hootchy-kootchy" dancer of better than usual taste.

A society matron saw St. Denis perform and raised a committee of twenty-five wealthy and prominent New Yorkers who rented the Hudson Theatre to stage a full program of St. Denis's dances, for which the dancer rushed into completion a third work, *The Incense*. Later, these early pieces were incorporated in her Indian panoramic dance suite: *Radha — The Temple, Incense — Purdah, Cobras — The Bazaar, Nautch — The Palace,* and *Yogi — The Forest*, which interpreted, according to St. Denis's ideas, various aspects of Indian life.

One of the New York impresarios who saw the Hudson Theatre program became St. Denis's agent and arranged tours for her in England and Europe. There St. Denis repeated the extraordinary success that had earlier come to the American dancer, Isadora Duncan.

As with Duncan, the Germans gave St. Denis adulation amounting to worship. The German Government offered to build a theatre as the foundation for St. Denis's art philosophy and to give her a home and a pension for life if she would remain in Germany. They saw in her interpretations of Eastern dance a philosophy that would revolutionize Western culture. Her theatre, they said, would become the focus for new ideas in dance, music, painting and sculpture. And St. Denis would have a stage on which to produce her works. Despite the temptation to head such an art foundation, St. Denis returned to America, well established by the European theatre as a major artist.

Her tours of the United States after her European triumph inspired a great number of young women and girls to dance professionally. The later influence and inspiration of the Russian prima ballerina Anna Pavlova on well-bred, college-educated Americans (one of whom was Agnes de Mille) brought a whole new class of dancers into American theatre. And at the close of World War II many of these were following in Duncan's and St. Denis's quest for Modern Dance.

St. Denis reached the artistic pinnacle of the European and American theatres with her mother in attendance as "Mother St. Denis," a title which abashed the most ardent male admirers of the "pagan goddess," as St. Denis was called.

The early period of her work was inspirational. She received "illumination" for her dance style from the Isis cigarette poster, and this led her to reading about Asiatic religions. Her brilliant intuition was the chief attribute of her "Oriental" phase. Later, St. Denis traveled abroad and observed the religious and court dances of India, China, Japan and Java, and studied the ancient cult of Assyria-Babylon.

It was as the "pagan goddess" and "the idol" that St. Denis became famous. She found a style of dance which marvelously expressed her romantic imagination, and she had the physical ability to personify a sinuous grace and a mysterious and seductive femininity. Her way to the top of her profession was aided not only by her mother but by many devoted friends, among them Stanford White, a famous man-about-town as well as a noted American architect and artist.

St. Denis was lovely and lovable and in later years wore the title "Miss Ruth" as the most beloved living dancer in the American theatre. In 1963, aged eighty-three (and sometimes, mischievously, pretending to be even older!) St. Denis was not only alive but active. She undertook a series of appearances on tour and was seen dancing on television programs, as well as talking about dancing.

Her second phase as a dancer was in sacred dance for Christian church denominations, in contrast to the dance of Eastern and so-called "pagan" religions. She made her home in Los Angeles, where her "Church of the Divine Dance" was established for her performances and the teaching of dance as a form of divine worship. Her work was greatly affected by her conversion to the Christian Scientist tenets of Mary Baker Eddy.

✎ Ted Shawn

Edwin Myers Shawn was born in Kansas, Missouri, in 1891, and lived in Denver, Colorado, in his teens. His father was a magazine and newspaper editor; his mother a Booth, a member of the famous acting family. When

Shawn was eleven, his mother and his older brother died within a few months of each other. His memories of his mother were colored by her interests in literature and drama. Mary Lee Booth Shawn had been a high school principal before her marriage, was the friend of writers and herself a book and drama reviewer. Shawn's family acted in amateur theatre productions, and he was cast from infancy in toddler's roles. After his mother's and brother's death and his father's remarriage, Shawn was a lonely boy. He consoled himself with books, reading two or three a day. At the age of fifteen, he estimated that he had read over five thousand books, and on a wide variety of subjects.

Dance was the furthest career from his mind and it was planned for him to enter the Methodist ministry. Living with his father and stepmother in Denver, Shawn graduated from high school and commenced university studies in theology. He contracted diphtheria and was given overdoses of an antitoxin, which paralyzed him. In the course of a long and painful convalescence he changed his mind about going to divinity school. A physician urged him to study dance as therapy for his paralyzed muscles, and Shawn began ballet under Hazel Wallack, an accomplished dancer and teacher and a pupil of Malvina Cavallazzi, who was the first director of the ballet school at New York's Metropolitan Opera House.

Shawn had always been athletic and he responded readily to dance training. He was of more than average height, over six feet tall, and not of the ballet *danseur* type in that day. He found the ballet admirable as discipline and made it the basis of a style for performance and teaching in later years.

Shawn did not fight his way into the theatre but danced into it. He fell in love with Hazel Wallack, proposed and became engaged. But Miss Wallack broke the engagement, and Shawn left Denver and went to Los Angeles. He worked as a stenographer for the city water works and continued studying dance even after he had fully regained physical fitness. Soon he turned all his strength and energy into dancing, exhilarated by his return to health and by the control dance exerted over his body. Gradually the broad possibilities of dance for religious worship, as church dance, appeared to him, creating the empathy which would spontaneously occur between him and St. Denis.

He spent the better part of his stenographer's wages on dance lessons and was invited by a ballet teacher, Norma Gould, to partner her. The great ballroom craze of the era, which developed the American taste for dance of the exhibition variety, was satisfied by "tango teas" in the afternoon and "supper club" dances after the theatre in the evening. Big hotels employed professional dancers to perform *thé dansant*.

Soon Shawn was on a split-second schedule that would have killed a weaker dancer. He worked, without a lunch break, for the Los Angeles City Water Department until 4:15 P.M. and then dashed to the Angelus Hotel to partner Norma Gould in the "tango teas." Then he rushed to a studio he had rented for a practice hall, and where he was soon teaching his ideas of dance to pupils who wanted instruction in "interpretive dancing." He and Norma Gould pooled their pupils to form a modest company and it was with this troupe that Shawn began working as choreographer for groups, while continuing to explore his solo capacities in dance. His creative work was done on weekends. Every evening by 10:05 he was changing into white tie and tails to step into the spotlight at the Alexandria Hotel with Miss Gould and dance for the supper set.

In his second summer in Los Angeles Shawn wrote a sketchy scenario and choreographed a pageant of dance for Gould, himself and other dancers for a movie, *The Dance of the Ages*, produced by the Thomas A. Edison film studio in Long Beach. It was done during Shawn's two-week vacation from the water works, and it netted him money which swelled his bank account. He was saving thriftily to go to New York and study under recognized masters of dance.

Dancing for therapy, dancing for exercise, dancing for fun and dancing to make some extra money were rapid stages in Shawn's development, and he passed through them to dance for an ideal that was all his own. He wanted to dance, and not only in the styles common to the era, of tap, ballroom, acrobatic and ballet. He read an article by the poet Bliss Carman, *The Making of a Personality*, which said things about dance that Shawn had been forming for himself out of his own feelings on dancing. He wrote Carman a fan letter, to which the poet replied suggesting that Shawn study with Mary Perry King in New Canaan, Connecticut. Mrs. King had collaborated as a dancer in two productions of Carman's in which the speaking voice in poetic recitation was the dance accompaniment.

To save traveling expenses, Shawn hired himself, Norma Gould and a troupe to the Santa Fe Railroad for a cross-country entertainment engagement. It was then the railroad's policy to provide recreation through entertainment for its workers, and Shawn danced for some of the toughest audiences he was ever to face — men who looked the prototypes of the grim-faced, two-gun pioneers who tamed the Wild West. He survived the experience and reached Connecticut. Soon thereafter, in New York, began his romance and collaboration with Ruth St. Denis.

In *One Thousand and One Night Stands* Shawn gave a vivid verbal picture of his personal and theatrical life from childhood through the Denishawn years.[29] These were the years when the school and company he established with his wife produced the first recognized academic study of dance and the famed trio of American Modern dancers: Graham, Humphrey and Weidman.

Shawn and St. Denis went separate ways after dissolving Denishawn in 1931, and Shawn developed two careers in the post-Denishawn years, either of which might have sufficed as a life work for a less energetic soul.

The first of these was his founding of his Men Dancers,

a company which he trained from 1931 and for which he composed a large repertoire. The troupe was active between the two world wars and danced across the American continent and abroad. It originated from Shawn's ideal of dancing for men, dance arts that were suited to masculine performers according to the physique, temperament and emotions of the male. This ideal he expounded in lectures and dance demonstrations for men in physical education colleges in American universities. He is the dean of dance lecturers and was instrumental in establishing dance within the college curriculum in America.

St. Denis and Shawn were the first dancers to be seriously accepted in American education. Today it is accepted that dance arts have a primary place within the fine arts and humanities curricula. But in 1916, when St. Denis and Shawn and their dancers appeared at the University of California's Greek Theatre in Berkeley, they were the first dancers to be let past the bar which had been raised by its board of trustees against dancers appearing at that college. Once, in Shreveport, Louisiana, a delegation of two hundred ministers and church elders marched on the city hall to protest "sacrilegious and blasphemous dancing" by the Denishawn dancers. Shawn refused to change the program, and when the performance began the audience was guarded in the theatre by the city's full police force. The program ended to general applause led by the mayor and other city officials.

However, after dance had come to be accepted as a major art in America, there remained strong prejudices against male dancers, and this Shawn was resolved to overcome. In autumn 1931 he attempted a tour with an all-male troupe, which was canceled halfway, joining many other similiar failures caused by the depression. At loose ends, without a school or company of his own (Denishawn had been terminated), Shawn returned to a former experiment which he had tried out in a summer school session for physical education at a state college in New York. It was to amplify masculine movement in athletics into dancing.

Physical education teachers were interested in Shawn's ideas, and he began to work, without salary, at Springfield College, Massachusetts, on an experimental program. He choreographed, as dance, movement which was special and essential to the male. In general, dancing was first choreographed and then men dancers were forced to adapt themselves to their roles. Shawn wished to develop a human and masculine approach to dance.

For example, he took the distinctive movements and individual rhythms of a specific sport and, with the collaboration of a musical composer-arranger, put the rhythms and patterns into suitable musical form.

His first pupils were as reluctant to dance as audiences across the United States were reluctant to look at men dancing. Most of these students knew nothing about dancing, but had built-in aversions, from the prejudice that dancing was effeminate, trivial and unworthy of a strapping, well-muscled male. It was considered poor taste for a man to participate in art forms of dance as a

hobby, and it was appalling for a man to consider dancing as a means of earning his living. However, Shawn
believed that if the American audience saw young native
athletes appearing in a masculine, not effeminate, repertoire, it would willingly accept the American male dancer
in the theatre. Shawn looked forward to the day when
dancing would be a profession and a career like any other
recognized and respected one for the man in America.

His first courses were taught to five hundred young
physical education students at Springfield College, which
graduated more than half the gymnasium and athletic
coaches in the country. Many of them also worked as
playground and camp recreation directors and so were
able to transfer Shawn's precepts about dance to younger
boys. Shawn avoided unfamiliar French terminology but
based his teaching on the ballet. He soon had his trucu-
lent students admitting that dancing was more strenuous
than training for football, basketball and wrestling. He
enjoyed the musical collaboration of Jess Meeker, a composer and arranger of excellence who was sympathetic to
Shawn's ideas. They made use of folk songs and spirituals,
music which was familiar and beloved in America. These
had the strong and rhythmic qualities Shawn wished to
express in dance, and he obtained effective results in
dance works of gusto and spirit. He also incorporated ordinary athletic activity, such as rowing a boat, into dance
patterns and rhythms. His dances based on work —
scything a field or using tools like the ax and the two-

handled saw — were arranged in similiar patterns and rhythms.

The initial course in dance at Springfield College was compulsory, not elective, and Shawn, as a result, drew students who would never have deigned to dance otherwise. The experimental program was a huge success, and from the enthusiasm it generated Shawn formed his all-male company at Jacob's Pillow, an old farmhouse and property he purchased in the early 1930s, when he believed himself retired from touring. It was near Springfield College, and Shawn continued to work at that institution, which is now affiliated with the academy of dance arts Shawn directs at Jacob's Pillow Dance Festival.

This Festival, the best known of its kind, was established in 1932, when Shawn had completed twenty-seven years of continuous touring as a performer and working as a choreographer and teacher. The Ted Shawn Theatre at Jacob's Pillow was opened in July 1942 and since 1953 has been an international dance center. In 1957 Shawn received the coveted Capezio Award for his contributions to the dance and was knighted by the King of Denmark, who conferred on Shawn the Cross of Dannebrog for his work in international dance.

Jacob's Pillow's dance curriculum for students is accredited by colleges, and since 1958 Shawn has taught a Rhythmic Choir course to church ministers and choir leaders. Although St. Denis and Shawn have lived and worked separately since the disbanding of Denishawn,

St. Denis frequently appears on Jacob's Pillow Dance Festival programs, and Shawn has been commentator for her solo concert performances. He remains active onstage, occasionally as dancer, sometimes as actor, but devotes himself full time to directing the school and theatre at Jacob's Pillow. He is a prolific writer, and his books and articles are among the most important literary contributions to the dance. His principles have been clearly and vividly expressed in his repertoire and in his books, articles and lectures.

Denishawn is the cradle and stronghold of Modern Dance in America. St. Denis and Shawn, although dissimiliar in dance styles, are the parent force of the dance.

"Denishawn dance" is a term loosely and illogically applied to some forms of Modern Dance. It is used by some writers to describe slightingly the "interpretative" styles which these writers find difficult to classify and impossible to systemize. The same pedantic attitude is taken toward "Duncan dance." In fact, as Duncan's dance had true substance and an unequaled power, so did "Denishawn dance" contain real pith and enormous influences.

As a school and company Denishawn set records that have never been surpassed, for it was entirely self-supporting for sixteen years, an autonomous academy of dance arts which never received a grant or subsidy but produced theatrical works of a scale then unknown for American ballet.

The principal dancers were St. Denis and Shawn,

who danced together and in solo. But Shawn was the prime teaching force. St. Denis had not taught before Denishawn, except to demonstrate her theories for an occasional private pupil. She and Shawn were compatible but not comparable as dancers and teachers.

St. Denis's approach to dance was feminine and intuitive. Shawn's was masculine, direct and pragmatic. St. Denis built her career on the mystery and seductiveness of the East. Shawn developed his on an aggressively masculine form and forte, frequently within American continental themes and from such ordinary subjects as American Negro spirituals, cowboys, and laborers. St. Denis was mercurial in temperament, naturally rhythmic, instinctively gifted for gesture and the usage of drapery in the dance. She was at her best teaching women of deeply feminine natures like her own. Shawn was far more mathematical and scientific, and he was very sensitive to the development of music along with the development of the dance.

Besides his work as a dancer, Shawn spent forty-five years studying and compiling theories of Delsarte's Applied Aesthetics, which he documented in a book called *Every Little Movement*. His students received from him teaching in ethnic dance, character dance, training according to the "schools" or systems of the French, Russian and Spanish classical dance, and his original contributions to the theory and composition of the free forms of Modern Dance. St. Denis's great development of Music Visualizations (which she worked on alone and with her pupil, Humphrey) originated in a classroom exercise conducted by Shawn, to Bach's *Inventions and Fugues*, which Shawn called the "contrapuntal" dance.[30]

Shawn's scientific approach to dance (for instance, in the masculine and the feminine approaches) and his basic Delsarte methods have given his teaching a discipline and force which his students, among them Graham, publicly acknowledge. Not the least of his gifts is his ability for discovering latent talent. He is the explorer of his era, insatiably curious about world dance, who discovered and introduced to American audiences a rich store of dancing in many individual artists and in the dance arts of many nations.

St. Denis, like Duncan, represents a romantic and idyllic dance spirit, and all her dancing, both "pagan" and "sacred," is essentially religious in character and idealistic of Woman. Her adaptations (some of which were unconscious) of Dalcroze Eurhythmics for Music Visualizations led to choric forms for Modern Dance.[31] Seeing Duncan in London, about 1900, was for St. Denis like beholding "the embodiment of cosmic rhythm," and she felt that Duncan diffused a powerful spirit, the outpouring of her own. But St. Denis never seemed to feel that she herself was a great teacher or an inspirational force, for she remarked that her students "quite probably missed the purpose of my rituals" but wound up with a technique, or "shell," that was usable in the theatre. Nevertheless, St. Denis is claimed as influence by many dancers, chiefly through the diffusion of her warm and kindling personality. Of these dancers Martha Graham is the greatest — although far from resembling St. Denis in temperament or style.

One of Denishawn's greatest contributions to the dance lay in the fact that its founders never subjugated the natural talents and instinctive powers of expression in their students. St. Denis, Shawn, Graham, Humphrey and Weidman are wholly individual. But they were all characteristically American, and so the American Modern Dance continued to develop a national style and content, while the German Modern Dance grew out of Dalcroze and Laban, Wigman and Jooss, and their compeers.

❧ III ❧

The Burgeoning

DUNCAN and St. Denis were contemporaries, but they represent separate eras in dance. The dancers emergent from Denishawn are the third generation in the dynasty of American Modern Dance. The most famous of these are Martha Graham, Doris Humphrey and Charles Weidman. Their influences are divided into two, one from Graham and the other from Humphrey and Weidman, who formed a company in which they collaborated as teachers and choreographers. Graham and Weidman were pupils of Shawn. Humphrey was St. Denis's protégée.

These three were not the only major dancers of their epoch. The important foreign graft for the American dance was in Hanya Holm. And there were several independent influences from dancers who did not belong to the Denishawn hierarchy, one of which came from Helen Tamiris. Modern Dance remained matriarchal, except for Shawn and Weidman, and, out of the Humphrey-Weidman school, José Limón.

Astonishing changes had occurred since Isadora set out

as prophet and priestess of the "new" dance. Unrelated but equally significant factors in science and philosophy altered social and artistic concepts. Bell's telephone, Edison's incandescent lamp and kinetoscope, and the new attitudes toward time and distance, from Einstein's statements about the theory of relativity to the developments in airplane and automobile travel, promised a brave new world. But on the heels of the Armistice came disillusion and cynicism. World War I failed to end wars, and the League of Nations, formed "to achieve international peace," was idealistic by nature but impotent in fact. Academic philosophy changed from the older Hegelian (from which modern idealism sprang) to a new philosophy influenced by logic and mathematics, in which Bertrand Russell was the historical figure. Romanticism, as had been represented by the philosophers Arthur Schopenhauer and Friedrich Nietzsche and the composer Richard Wagner, gave way to Modernism, a term applied to the functional and utilitarian. The epoch which began for the dance in the 1920s was marked by radical thought and strong international currents in politics as well as in the arts. The epoch produced a wholly new philosophy for Modern Dance which became, in fact, the social conscience of its times.

Jooss's ballet *The Green Table* commented on contemporary politicians, and Wigman's dance style, angular, dynamic and percussive, was the antithesis of Duncan's "harmony with Nature." A fierce new rebellion agitated the twentieth-century dance against Beauty, which seemed curiously outdated after World War I. Isadora had preached that the dance would bring Beauty back into the world. Her postwar successors looked to the dance to describe harsh realities and the inhuman tyrannies which caused human suffering.

In the somber mood which affected the arts, the former ideal of elegance, in a Victorian and Edwardian age, was replaced by one of functionalism. Modernism swept the plush sofa and charming bric-a-brac from the drawing room and replaced these with starkly essential furnishings after the styles of Eero Saarinen and Charles Eames. The change in the dance was as abrupt and startling. Modern Dance, which was founded on philosophies and in fact (through dancers like Duncan, Graham and Humphrey) owed some of its form to academic philosophic ideas, adopted a characteristic of twentieth-century philosophy — logic, as well as feeling.

The "dance of experience" became totally real, and times were bad. Martha Graham saw through the eye of anguish, first person singular, but it was the eye of genius. Others, less gifted, followed the vogue in functional dance, making a precept to deny all grace and beauty, sweetness and joy. For a time, Modern Dance was in serious danger of losing its vitality and its dynamic character. As the utilitarian propaganda dance it was more tool than art form.

Dancers eager to find "a cause" sought the ills of the period, and these included the Nazi, Fascist, anti-Semitic, anti-Negro, anti-labor factions. Becoming the dance of angry protest, Modern Dance was sarcastically called "pink" dancing, from the term applied to left-wing politics accused of "red" or bolshevist tendencies. In concert halls dancers no longer lyrically sought harmony with Nature and Beauty but made violent and sometimes obtuse statements about the state of the world. "Modern dance is being performed in dark dungeon," commented a critic, making a pun on the state of mind and the dimly lit halls in which the dance was being seen at this time. In its era of "gloom and doom" Communists made a shrewd bid to enlist the radical American Modern Dance. The artists, although sympathetic and indignant about social ills, were not easily conscripted for political propaganda. Their dedication, in a word, was to dance. But dissention within the new dance forced some dancers into opposing camps. Those who admired Graham complained that Weidman was too frivolous, and they considered Humphrey mystical. Many were drawn to the German dance, and for these Holm was the chief pedagogue. Largely emergent from the Holm school were dancers who avowed themselves against the current styles of American dance, as represented in Graham and Humphrey and Weidman. One of the precepts of the new ideology was to make dance a vehicle for the mass, not an art for individual expression and the autonomous dancer's fame.

The ideal of "mass" dancing came from Germany, and young American dancers believed that they could utilize the dance as a revolt against political and social ills.

They were also against the increasing symbolism of the American Modern Dance. Graham, they said, was ambiguous and abstract and locked within her own "cavern of the heart." The crusading dancers would mass, in themselves, to move the dance directly into the masses, the proletariat. They meant by "the masses" the American audience en masse, the large, tolerant but exceedingly independent and opinionated body better known as "the general public." Burning to change the wrongs of the world, the young dancers gave performances in trade union halls for labor groups and made a point of joining themselves within the Worker's Dance League. Minority groups versus capitalists was the common dance theme, explored in pieces titled *Eviction, Hunger, Unemployment, Well Fed, Homeless Girl,* and *While Waiting for Relief.* Timely and intensely dreary, this repertoire depressed the audience while it exhilarated the militant dancers. Coincidentally, ballet had a resurgent popularity in the United States through the Ballet Russe de Monte Carlo, which became a resident American company in the 1930s. The classical repertoire and technique dazzled the American theatregoer. While indignant Modern dancers strove to dance "the truth," audiences flocked to see the ballerinas of the Ballet Russe perform ravishing pirouettes and a breathless series of *fouettés*. Obviously, the proletariat preferred the scene of a frothy Massine "champagne" ballet to the "dungeon" of the "new" dance.

The totality of the "mass dance" overshot its mark.

Audiences were stupefied with boredom or bewildered by esoteric "realism." The American audience still persisted in attending the theatre to be entertained, refusing to be preached at from the stage. The socialist and "pink" era of the dance was short and abortive, and the only dancers who survived were those who were creative, and whose energy and strength matched their imagination and skill.

Another and far more influential factor in this era was that of the academic dance. In 1926 the first dance major to be offered college students was established at the University of Wisconsin, as the result of the work of Margaret H'Doubler. This enterprising woman determined to treat dance as a college subject, "philosophical, analytical, and creative," thus laying the foundation for the academic dance today. Students, most of them studying for a teacher's certificate in physical education, attended summer courses in dance at the University of Wisconsin, and one of these was Martha Hill. She had studied under Anna Duncan, one of Isadora's protégées, and was trained in ballet, music and Dalcroze Eurhythmics. In 1930-1931 Hill was a member of Martha Graham's concert troupe. Far more than the average physical education major Martha Hill understood and appreciated training in dance.

Hill was head of the Physical Education Department at New York University and in the summer of 1934 went to head the Bennington School of Dance at Bennington College.

Physical education had been making use of dance as a

functional or physical exercise. Artistically, college or conservatory dance leaned heavily to "expressional" dance, commonly (and most often incorrectly) dubbed "Duncanesque" dance. Scarf and garland dancers recklessly improvised movement without pattern or style, and it was against the artless dance (dance as self-expressive "play") that the serious Modern dancers rebelled. *To a Wild Rose, The Lilies, Winds at Evening, The Brook* and others of this caste had driven many dancers into the tenement school of "proletariat" dance in revulsion from the same simpering artifice against which Isadora Duncan revolted.

At Bennington, the dance was not pretty posturing but an art form with style. These dance courses originated from a plan of Mary Josephine Shelly, the administrative director of student activities at the University of Chicago. She suggested a comprehensive course in dance, and Modern Dance as the best source of training and creative style. Bennington College's summer course began with one hundred students, with Martha Hill teaching technique and composition. Professional dancers were invited to inaugurate college workshops, and the academic foundation of Modern Dance was thus established.

College dance had been "barefoot dancing" at its most naive, and a girlish adventure in physical education. Under the professional dancers Graham, Humphrey, Weidman, and Holm, Bennington became the fount of vigorous experiments in dance education. The fourth generation of American Modern dancers emerged from this era, many of them out of Bennington.

The assessment of college dance in the United States has not yet been made, but it is certain that the period affectionately referred to as "the Bennington years" was very important for the dance in America. Modern Dance as yet had no subsidy (it later received grants from private patrons and cultural groups), and its early rebellious existence was precarious and penurious. Even the glamorous Isadora worked hard in order to dance. The Modern dancers emergent in the 1930s ploughed their way onstage and worked themselves to a state of physical exhaustion, struggling against apathy and ridicule to communicate philosophies and dance idioms which were strange and new. They were, in the real meaning of the word, pioneers. They adventured farther in analysis and technical aspects of the dance and more radically in the dance's philosophy than Isadora had done, but with no less spirit and dedication. As the seed of inspiration was Isadora, and Denishawn the equable climate in which it grew, it is to the dancers who followed them that we look for the burgeoning of Modern Dance's genius.

Martha Graham

Denishawn's dance curriculum stretched to suit its founders' experiments in dance, and was pliant enough

to provide incentive for pupils of widely varying styles.
But in 1915 a student turned up at the handsome property on Sixth Street, Los Angeles, who seemed unlikely
to fit into Denishawn.

This was Martha Graham. Born in 1893 near Pitts-
burgh, Pennsylvania, she moved to California as a child
with her parents and a sister, Jeordie. Dr. Graham was a
neurologist, a severe man who brought his children up
with strict discipline. He told his daughters that he always knew when they were lying because their muscles
involuntarily betrayed them. Martha never forgot this,
and as a dancer she described the dance as "a graph of
the heart." This was the Modern pioneer whose work
propounded the dynamic principle for American contemporary dance. She established her thesis for dance
on *motor memory*, the nervous system, which, to Graham, subconsciously connects the living person with an-
cestral moods. By inquiring and discovering these, the
dancer finds an explanation of what we are in our own
time.

Plato led Graham to the belief that mythology was
the psychology of the ancients, and that within the legendary lore of past civilizations the dancer could find
symbols common to the human race and universal to it.
The "graph of the heart" was therefore the common de-
nominator of human moods, and, often, the explanation
of our actions.

Martha Graham was not a pretty child with winning
ways, and she was not a lovely, graceful young woman,

as her predecessors, Duncan and St. Denis, had been. Graham's life was in no way like the lives of her artistic forbears. As a child, Isadora was allowed extraordinary freedom, and she believed that this early liberation from strict and conventional propriety (then the custom in rearing children) inspired her "free" dance. Martha Graham was an obedient child, submissive to a strict upbringing. Ruth St. Denis had an idyllic childhood, which she described as "enchanted." Her mother's boundless faith in her was the direct source of her success, and she adored her father, who was a visionary. Martha Graham's relationships with her parents were correct but not warm. Her father disapproved of the theatre, and Graham waited until after his death to persuade her mother to let her study dance at Denishawn.

But Martha Graham was a performer from infancy, when she danced down the aisle of a church during service. The Grahams were of Puritan and Presbyterian faiths and New England stock, and Mrs. Graham a descendant of Miles Standish. The family was conservative, and Martha's audiences were the patients in her father's waiting room and the servants in her mother's kitchen. In her junior year in high school she saw St. Denis at a concert and later wrote: "Miss Ruth opened a door for me and I passed through it." But she had no idea of what direction to take in dance when she entered Denishawn.

She at first studied under St. Denis, her idol, but St. Denis was of the opinion that she could not teach Martha. She asked Shawn to try the new student in his classes. Shawn accepted Martha. She had had no previous training in rhythmic movement and she was older than the majority of beginning dance students. She had no immediately perceptible gifts for dancing. But Shawn was a patient teacher, and a sympathetic one. He, too, had come late to dancing and from actual physical paralysis, and he admired grit and diligence in others. Graham was as diligent as Shawn was patient. "From the first," Shawn comments, "Martha was conspicuous for her appetite for hard work."

They persevered for two years, and in the dance *Serenata Morisca*, which he was setting for the class, Shawn saw a glimpse of Graham's dynamic personality. He dates that as the birth of Graham as a dancer. So impressed was he that he offered to give her lessons without charge if she would promise him to work hard and without stint of herself. She was later, from 1919 to 1921, his assistant and a teacher at the Ted Shawn Studio. In her autobiography, *An Unfinished Life*, St. Denis wrote "[Martha Graham] owes her professional development to the deep concern and affection that Ted had for her during those early years."

As Graham was later to say, Shawn taught her discipline and gave her courage to be herself without compromise. She idolized St. Denis and she had been inspired to study dance from seeing St. Denis perform. But St. Denis was a beautiful woman and a dancer in the

romantic style. Graham was not physically or tempera-
mentally suited to romantic dance. In Denishawn,
among lovely, lithe girls, she seemed awkward. No one,
least of all Graham, dreamed that she was a bird of eagle
character who would soar boldly and to immense heights
in the dance.

Shawn made her his partner and choreographed several works for her, among them *Xochitl*, the love story of
a maiden of the ancient Toltec civilization.[32] One of the
dancers in this ballet, a major success in the Denishawn
repertoire, was Charles Weidman, another pupil and protégé of Shawn's. Shawn toured from Los Angeles to New
York with a troupe which included Graham and Weidman. Martha Graham was the leading female soloist, and
she danced everything from Music Visualization works
choreographed by Shawn to "Barbaric Suites." [33] The
comprehensiveness of this dance education might have
confused a lesser artist but served only to enrich Graham.
She never stopped learning. From St. Denis she learned
the masterly use of drapery and lighting which St. Denis,
in turn, owed to Fuller.

Louis Horst, another of the great influences to emerge
from Denishawn, became Graham's close friend in her
formative years and the guiding influence of her early
work. Horst was born in Kansas City, Missouri. He studied piano and violin in San Francisco and theory in Vienna. It was in 1915 while he was playing the piano in a
vaudeville house that the Denishawn Company hired

him as accompanist for ten days. He stayed with the company ten years, while it was developing the great original artists Graham, Humphrey and Weidman.

He traveled to Europe and brought back descriptions and photographs of Mary Wigman's new dance, which he showed to Graham. These pictures were her first inkling of Wigman's work, with which Graham's was later compared. When Graham left Denishawn, Horst became her close associate. In her words, he created a landscape for her to move in.

Hired by dancers to be accompanist and arranger, Horst inevitably became their protector. He was wholly lacking in personal ambition, although he was an inventive composer. He was part tyrant, part slave to the dancers he bullied and cherished in his long career. Almost every major concert dancer — including St. Denis, Shawn, Graham, Humphrey, Weidman, Tamiris, Kreutzberg, Page and de Mille — was indebted to Horst. He died at the age of eighty in 1964.

Serving as Graham's musical director from 1926 to 1948, he composed several scores for her works, including *Primitive Mysteries, American Provincials, Frontier* and *El Penitente*. He interested her in primitive music, which led to her work, in the 1930s, with American Indian material and in characteristic American behavior patterns.

Horst was conductor for the ballet company of Adolph Bolm (who organized the ballet companies of the New York Metropolitan Opera, the Chicago Civic Opera and

Isadora Duncan, about 1903.

Ruth St. Denis (with two unidentified dancers) in *Egypta,* 1910.

Photograph by Sarony.

Ted Shawn in *Prometheus Bound*, 1929.

Photograph by John Lindquist.

Martha Graham in *Night Journey*, 1948.

Doris Humphrey and Charles Weidman in *New Dance*, 1935.

Photograph by Thomas Bouchard.

Hanya Holm in *Trends*, 1937.

Photograph by Barbara Morgan.

Helen Tamiris in *Negro Spirituals*, about 1930.

Photograph by Marcus Blechman.

Carmen de Lavallade, student of Lester Horton and Carmelita Maracci, with Glen Tetley in *Carmina Burana,* choreographed by John Butler to Carl Orff's cantata for the New York City Opera, 1959.

Photograph by Jack Mitchell.

the San Francisco Ballet), but after joining Graham he became primarily concerned with Modern Dance. Until his death he taught weekly classes at New York's Neighborhood Playhouse, the Juilliard School, and Martha Graham's School of Contemporary Dance.

He was uncompromising in his approach to dance, discouraging improvisation and insisting that every dance work must have a valid and recognizable form as art. These principles influenced Martha Graham and gave to her work a toughness of fibre and a positive form lacking in the amorphous style of a great many of her contemporaries. No other non-dancer so directly influenced the American dance as did Louis Horst.[34]

Martha Graham danced with the Denishawn Company until 1923 and left to work for the Greenwich Follies Revue. In 1925 she was hired by the Eastman School of Music, Rochester, New York, to teach music and drama students. She began to experiment with movement instead of teaching known dance forms and, so doing, she created a vocabulary all her own, for the dance.

She returned to natural movement — walking, running, leaping. Gradually, she formed a technique, developing this on her physical and psychological response to the dance impulse. Like Duncan, Martha Graham was an original dancer, but Duncan sought for a free and natural movement which was lyrical. Martha Graham sought for dance as the expression of the human self. She was very sensitive to her times, and her subject matter was realistic, not romantic. Some human emotions were not conventionally pretty; therefore some movements in the Graham dance would be as tortured as the tormented human heart. Some natural movements appeared uncouth to the romanticists in the audience, but if they were real and true Graham would make use of them for the purpose of expressing her meaning in dance.

Her first New York concert held echoes of Denishawn. This program, in 1926, included A *Study in Lacquer*, *Danse Languide*, *Tanagra*, *Danse Rococo* and *Gypsy Portrait*. Wrapped in a brocade sari, her hair in a sleek coil, she danced *Three Poems to the East*, something St. Denis might have performed. But in 1927 she broke with this influence in a work called *Revolt*, and for a time she was a martyr to austerity in dance, as though to deny all beauty and romance.

Her work met with outraged criticism. Few in the general audience understood what she was trying to interpret, and many accused her of deliberately debasing the dance and insulting the human race. Martha Graham believed hat the artist must destroy himself before he could crete. This meant separating herself from all former influences and emerging new and purified from the wrenching ordeal.

At this stage of Modern Dance development the times were neither easy nor tranquil. International political anarchy and religious and scientific schisms kept the world in an uproar. In the United States, the stock market crash of 1929, resulting in the American depression, was followed by the national banking crisis in 1933. The Spanish Civil War broke out in 1936.

In Germany, the Wigman influence entirely superseded those of Duncan and St. Denis, but in America a number of facile dancers strove to preserve the Duncanesque style. The American dancers were almost always blithe and lissome, nymphs with flower garlands and gossamer scarves, but Martha Graham was repelled by the merely ornamental. She stripped her dance of all decorative and superfluous movement. Much of her theme and characterization was agonized rather than idealized.

Her will and purpose were inflexible. She refused to dance what she did not believe, simply to make herself popular with the audience. "I do not want to dance as a tree, a flower or a wave," she cried. She wished to dance "something of the miracle that is a human being." To do this, she had to break through the seemingly unending frieze of feminine beauty which stretched into Modern Dance from Isadora and St. Denis, and into the ballet from exquisite ballerinas like Pavlova. In musical terms, these were violins and oboes, mellow, sweet and gracious, and Graham was a strident and percussive instrument. She danced anguish and terror, hate and woe. The age was no longer one of golden freedom but of anger and despair. Jazz was shrilling "the blues" and Graham's style had the staccato impulses of the era, and a fierce, compelling identity.[35]

In 1930 she danced at the Metropolitan Opera House,

New York, as the Sacrifice in Massine's ballet to Stravinsky's *Rite of Spring*. The following year she presented her first major work, *Primitive Mysteries*. Amazingly prolific as a choreographer (Martha Graham has composed more than one hundred and fifty works and is still composing), she soon established a large repertoire and attracted a great deal of notice. Audiences quarreled in theatre lobbies after she danced, and lively wars were waged in the press. Mrs. Graham was bewildered by denunciation of her daughter's dance. She wondered why people said terrible things about Martha, who was "such a sweet, old-fashioned girl." Martha Graham was never to be the idol of the general audience, but she began to reach a discerning group who recognized what she was expressing and the genius with which she was interpreting her themes and ideas. Renouncing a private life, Graham devoted herself to the dance. She was married for a time to a dancer, Erick Hawkins. The marriage ended in divorce, and Graham devoted herself to one career — that of the dancer.

While she was creating her early repertoire, finding a dance vocabulary and learning to express herself in it, she seemed tormented. The general audience called Martha Graham a freakish dancer. She was named the "dark soul" of the American dance. Her friends could only offer their friendship; no one could help her find herself and her way of dance. These friends were few, but they were loyal to their faith in Graham as a great artist. Among them were Louis Horst, who was her chief guide and mentor in this period; Agnes de Mille, who, as a dancer, was sympathetic with Martha's struggle to choreograph; and two discerning critics, Martin of the New York *Times* and Watkins of the New York *Herald Tribune*. She drew to herself a company of fine dancers, who became, by the 1960s, the most magnificent dance unit in the country.

In 1936 Graham was invited by the Nazi Government to perform in Germany for the Olympic Games. She was offered a large sum of money, but better still, the opportunity for her dance to attract worldwide attention at the Games. Graham refused the invitation because the Nazis were anti-Semitic, and half Graham's company was Jewish. She would not dance in a country where the government treated Jews with contempt.

"But Miss Graham is not herself a Jew, is she?" asked a surprised Nazi official. No, but Miss Graham's personal idealogy refuted the persecution of persons for reasons of religious faith or nationality.

"It would be bad for America," said the Nazi official, "if American dance is not represented by its greatest artist!"

"It would be bad for you," retorted Graham, "because everyone will know exactly why!" No dancer from America went to Germany to perform at the Olympic Games.[36]

Primitive Mysteries, the first Graham masterpiece, was her sixty-third composition. At this phase the Graham dance was experimental. She saw herself as being "in a state of innocence" and she was determined not to depend on conventional inspirations of musical rhythms and moods. She seemed to dance *against* instead of *to* music. From this came a syncopation for dance which affected the contemporary ballet. She declared: *Dance is an absolute*; and the "pure dance" school received a further impression and development from her.

Graham evolved an explanation for her dance. Its basis was human effort, and she thought of this as "life." She saw this force or energy as starting in the nerve centers and as coursing through the body from percussive impulses. She imagined that such impulse flowing through the body into arms and legs (as movement animates a whip) would produce a tremendous vitality in dance. She called these impulses "contractions" and explored them through the normal act of breathing. When the dancer exhaled, his torso contracted; when he inhaled, his torso lifted or was released.[37]

Ballet spurns the ground, and ballet *danseurs* balance themselves in perfect aplomb or leap with apparent effortlessness into the air. Graham utilized the ground and incorporated it into the dance by suspensions and falls, thinking of knees and thighs as hinges for the body down to and up from the ground. Graham's dancers were not nymphs and gods of wind and sea and tree but mortals, in movement earthy and earthbound. The style, or vocabulary, of Graham's dance was not a willful rebellion against other and older forms, but the clearest expression of her dance's content and meaning. Her area of exploration stretched into the extremities of experience, far beyond bounds set by "good taste" in the conventional society where manners and mores are made. The Graham dance was startling and depressing, terribly serious and intimate. Like the poet William Butler Yeats, Graham believed that mankind's gravest issues lay in sex and death.

Following no style, she made her own patterns of movement. These were, essentially, natural movements, but her choreography strangely distorted and emphasized leaps, leg and arm stretches, muscular articulations of the hips, and especially falls and crawls. The Chorus of the Daughters of the Night in *Night Journey* is a prime example of Graham's use of the floor. The dancers pulsate with contraction and release and their synchronized leaps are based on the same impulses. Graham begins the action with a series of falls which uniquely illustrate Modern Dance's integration of the earth into the essentially aerial nature of the dance.

A dancer's timing and projection are as innate as physical size and shape. Graham's personal style was an invention for the dance as definite as though she were a writer evolving a new compositional form in literature. Her extraordinary muscular control was inspired by her psychical sense of the dance, which she saw as stemming from the life current. She said, "Every dance is a kind of fever chart, a graph of the heart." She was intensely feminist and she seemed to have a private, gnawing sorrow, unutterable in words, which she tersely and cryptically translated in dance. She was intensely moral, and only an ironic wit saved her from becoming preachy. And through an intellectual grasp of her art she learned to use "life current" as percussive and dynamic impulses of energy.

When she was compared to Wigman because she used acrobatic techniques and soul-searing themes, Graham retorted that she had never studied in the German school. She left Denishawn before Wallman arrived to teach German technique. Graham insisted that German and American dance differed because the dancers' roots were different. Modern Dance did not possess a codified technique nor absolute aesthetic form. It was evoked through movements that, disjointed in themselves, combined in phrasing to express, with the body, the inner self. *Modern Dance was a state of mind before it became a way of moving.* Graham now set herself the task of evolving academics for her dance. She had very strong thighs, a wonderfully pliant back and feet of unusual flexibility, long arms and a supple neck, an exquisitely molded head. She kicked straight up in a "split" of an astonishing 180 degrees and she could inch a foot across the floor with a serpentine undulation. With her own body as her laboratory, Graham perfected one of the definitive techniques of Modern Dance.

Sensitive to the modern world, Graham at first danced as she saw life, "nervous, sharp, zigzag," but as her functional technique was perfected she began to explore the world in wider scope, and developed her phenomenal insight into the ritual and emotion which bind peoples of all nations and all ages as one human race. *Frenetic*

Rhythms (1933), dances of possession, was followed by chronicles of significant events composed in the 1930s: *American Provincials, Frontier, Horizons* and *American Document.* In this decade, Graham became widely known. She not only danced but choreographed, directed and produced for the theatre, and with eminent people like Katharine Cornell and Archibald MacLeish.

She showed a widening range, from the satirical *Every Soul Is a Circus* (1939), a study of a frivolous, foolish woman, to her most joyous and universally beloved work, *Appalachian Spring* (1944), with the Aaron Copland score. *Dark Meadow* (1946), a profound and lyrical work, returned to primitive ritual; *Eye of Anguish* (1950) was the heroic tragedy of King Lear; and *Seraphic Dialogue* (1955), the beatific vision of Joan of Arc. There were others and in different veins: *Diversion of Angels* (1948) and *Canticles for Innocent Comedians* (1952). Her genius was abundant and kaleidoscopic, her invention original and strong. Who but Martha Graham would have composed both *Clytemnestra* and *Acrobats of God,* or *Appalachian Spring* and *Phaedra*? But it is with works of the character of *Clytemnestra* that Graham's genius is most acknowledged. This is the apex of her grand dance design in ancient Greek drama.

Martha Graham began her mythological repertoire in *Tragic Patterns* (1933) or perhaps before that, in *Alceste* (1926), danced to the Gluck music from the opera of the Euripides tragedy. No one, not even Martha Graham, then knew that she would reform the theatre dance as

Gluck had reformed opera. As St. Denis had been drawn to the East and its mystery and sinuous grace, so was Graham drawn to ancient Greece, and its cruel valor and violent but poetic justice. Graham said that she saw herself as building a new pantheon, or habitation for the gods, and in it she showed demons as well as divinities. She did this through her study of psychological impulses and acts, and a masterly use of symbolism in dance, especially dramatic in her Greek repertoire.

Her evocation of the classical world commenced with *Herodiade* (1944), Graham's one-hundred-and-ninth composition. It continued into *Cave of the Heart,* the story of Media and Jason; *Errand into the Maze,* the Minotaur legend; *Night Journey,* the Oedipus myth, in which Graham was Queen Jocasta; and *Alcestis,* a rite of spring, with characterizations of King Admetus and Queen Alcestis. In 1958, *Clytemnestra,* the largest work, was hailed as a masterpiece. It was followed by *Phaedra* (1962) and *Circe* (1963).

Graham was a small woman, about five feet three inches tall, with dense dark hair, a bony sculptured face and what has been described as a perpetually haunted expression. She looked like a woman who saw visions, and her magic lay in her art of making these visions visible onstage for the audience. Her magical ability to transform herself into the characters she choreographed made Martha Graham tall and majestic as the mythological queens, or stooped and anguished as a suffering woman. She could be full of grandeur or wicked satire;

mystical, exalted, sublimely pure and good, or possessed by evil, and evilly possessive. Sometimes her characters were rapt, veiled, symbolic; other characters had the crude energy of elemental truths. Her Mary of Scotland in *Episodes*, a work in collaboration with George Balanchine of the New York City Ballet, was a moving dance portrait of the unhappy queen.

Martha Graham in the 1960s is the superb iconoclast of the dance, the most successful and productive of all living Modern dancers. She is completely successful not only in her renown but because she refused to alter her style or qualify her convictions. She has been accepted on her own terms, and the dance technique she invented has set precedents for dancers in all forms of dance. "Technically speaking," says Agnes de Mille, "Graham's is the single largest contribution in the history of Western dancing."

Graham's first two appearances in England made little impression on the British theatre, where Modern Dance was largely unknown. Ignorant of the developments of the American Modern Dance style, British audiences found Graham's works ugly or obtuse. Then in 1963 Graham took her company to the Edinburgh Festival and to London, where *Circe* received its world premiere, and Graham was hailed by the British audience as a great dance innovator. Audiences now knew a great deal more about world dance, many influential British critics had written enthusiastic praise of Graham's genius. Above all, Graham's matchless company danced with such passion and skill that it was rapturously acclaimed. Its inspiration at once influenced British dancers.[38]

She never became a popular artist. Many of her great works needed to be seen several times before they were clear and meaningful. And she did not cease to shock those who sought dancing which was conventionally pretty. Into 1963 she was still affronting some audiences, and two members of Congress protested the inclusion of Graham's works in theatrical presentations sent abroad by the United States Cultural Exchange Program.[39] But by now Graham's prestige lifted her far above individual prejudice.

Graham became more serene and patient, although never less positive. In her foreign tours she opened her company classes to the public for its better awareness of her principles and techniques. She is a literate and articulate woman who has meticulously explained her philosophy for dance.

As a choreographer she has created a magnificent repertoire. As a dancer she had a very personal way of moving, so strikingly individual that it is doubtful if the roles she created will ever be satisfactorily re-created. But she has trained and developed some of the most exciting dancers of the day.

Her productions have been enhanced by the music of composers Horst and Copland, Samuel Barber and Paul Hindemith. Notable artists such as the Japanese Isamu Noguchi have designed her sets. Graham's work as a fine costume designer added considerably to the visual impact of her dance. She directs the Martha Graham School of Contemporary Dance, Inc., in New York, appears regularly in Broadway seasons under the sponsorship of the Rothschild Foundation, and has been called "the greatest single ambassador we have ever sent to Asia." In 1957, twenty-one years after she rejected the Nazi Government's invitation to dance in Germany, she danced her premiere *Judith* in Berlin, to dedicate the Benjamin Franklin Congress Hall in that city. The "dark soul" of the American contemporary dance became its most brilliant light. She has held two Guggenheim Fellowships, and was the first dancer to be awarded one.

Graham's influence is wide and strong on the theatre dance and will undoubtedly continue after her own career ends, in the precepts of her teaching and through the dancers she has trained. These include Jane Dudley, Mary Hinkson, Pearl Lang, Helen McGehee, Sophie Maslow, May O'Donnell, Matt Turney, Ethel Winter, Yuriko, John Butler, Robert Cohan, Merce Cunningham, Erick Hawkins, Stuart Hodes, Bertram Ross and Glen Tetley. Her most celebrated protégée is Pearl Lang, a beautiful, lyrical dancer who is a noted choreographer. Merce Cunningham is the most controversial male dancer of our era. His experimental dances with the modern composer John Cage have been variously described as sinister, inspired, decadent and evolutionary.

In 1956 Martha Graham made a summation of her work on film, *A Dancer's World*, which is now a part of classroom study as well as a film classic. In 1958 and

1960 two more films were made, of *Appalachian Spring* and *Night Journey*, and a film is planned to show a representative repertoire of Graham's works, danced under her supervision by dancers she has trained, in order to preserve them in their original form.

Graham has said that her concern is for the subtle being (the I and You) who lies in the subtle body, beneath the gross muscles. In setting the *subtle being* free she became the acknowledged genius of the contemporary dance. Graham influenced the dance in a way that neither Duncan nor St. Denis could — Graham made it possible for women without personal beauty and obvious charm to dare to dance. Graham earned a spare and ageless beauty from her work, but her first and almost impossible task was to win acceptance from the audience for her style of dancing and her type of dancer.

Graham did this at a time when Modern Dance in America was competing with a ballet renaissance led by foreign ballerinas like the bewitching Alexandra Danilova and the romantic Alicia Markova. Audiences who admired Sugarplum Fairies and Swan Queens were more shocked than attracted by the characterizations of Graham's imagination. The ballet idealized the human form and relied on poetic drama. Graham's dancing was full of emotional pain and deliberately accented physical strain of movement. She declared that the audience must see itself in the dance, must identify with the dancers, not as exotic creatures of myth or fantasy but as "something of the miracle that is the human being." Almost imperceptibly, she began to grip the heart and mind of the American audience. In that audience she communicated most immediately and vividly with girls and women, making them conscious that they were not fairy queens but mortal and alive in the inner self. She called so intimately and passionately to so many that her technique became the most widely known of the Modern style. It is internationally recognized and in Europe is called *exercises de style*. Her New York school is now the mecca of Modern Dance for foreign dancers, among these the traditionally classical dancers of the Russian ballet.

No dancer worked with less encouragement and against more scathing criticism than Graham. None persisted in a philosophy of dance with more integrity. Graham's success is proof that while criticism at its best may prove stimulating and constructive, it is never essential to creative development. Her example is not for dancers alone but for all who dare to make the human effort that is life.

✍ Doris Humphrey and Charles Weidman

Doris Humphrey was of New England stock, a lineal descendant of William Brewster, elder of the Pilgrim Church in the early colony of Massachusetts, and of the poet and essayist Ralph Waldo Emerson. Her two grandfathers were ministers of the Congregational Church, and she was brought up in a devoutly religious home where the Sabbath was strictly kept. But the aesthetic part of life was not neglected, and Doris's parents encouraged her to cultivate a love for theatre arts. Her father was a professional photographer, her mother a pianist. They sent Doris to dancing school when she was eight and were delighted that the little girl showed marked talent.

Doris attended the Parker School in Chicago, studied ballet under Mary Wood Hinman, and was also trained in ballroom dance, folk forms, "expressional" or Duncanesque dance, and "clog," a popular tap dance in wooden-soled shoes. She continued her ballet training under excellent teachers in Chicago, Josephine Hatlanek, a ballet mistress from Vienna, and two well-known Russians, Serge Oukrainsky and Andreas Pavley.

While in high school, she saw a performance by the Anna Pavlova company. Pavlova bewitched the young Doris, as she bewitched so many girls and young women of the day. Agnes de Mille wrote, on seeing Pavlova: "My life was wholly altered by her." So, too, was Doris Humphrey's. The Pavlova company danced for a short season in Chicago, and Doris attended every performance, even those given on Sundays. At seventeen, still a schoolgirl, Doris choreographed her first work: *Persephone and Demeter*, the theme of the Greek allegory of winter and spring. She danced for charity benefits, soirées and garden parties, and her beauty and grace enchanted audiences. After completing high school, she taught danc-

ing, continuing with irregular professional engagements
— some for the Santa Fe Railroad, the same unlikely impresario that had employed the Ted Shawn Dancers. Her
specialty was a "cartwheel" dance, a feat of rhythmic
acrobatics not unlike the dancing that Ruth St. Denis
had performed for Worth's in New York. The "adagio"
style of exhibitionist dance was very popular and was
generally construed as superlative "ballet."

Doris's main objective was teaching, and because she
wished to teach a comprehensive curriculum she decided
to study at Denishawn, then the mecca for American
dancers. She applied for admission, was accepted, and
entered Denishawn in 1917, aged twenty-two. "Doris
appeared at Denishawn," recalls a contemporary, "looking like the popular idea of a schoolmarm. She wore severe clothes, a plain, dark skirt and a starched shirtwaist,
high at the neck, tight at the wrist. Her hair was brushed
until it shone, but it was bundled into a tight knot. And
she was so stiff and staid she looked a prim old maid. She
was the least likely person to be taken for a dancer —
until she began to dance."

When this timid, respectful schoolmarm type appeared
in class St. Denis at once recognized her potentiality as a
dancer. Thanks to her long training in dance and her own
musicality, Doris could move like a nymph. She had the
body of a nymph, lithe, strong, flexible and lyrical. She
was no ordinary student, and St. Denis not only taught
her, she also made her a member of the Denishawn company.

St. Denis was Doris's inspiration and St. Denis willingly responded as teacher and guide. She and Doris collaborated on *Tragica*, the first contemporary American work danced without conventional musical accompaniment. St. Denis encouraged Doris to choreograph as well as dance and she developed Doris's talent for lyricism in the Music Visualizations. Doris was an indispensable dancer in the St. Denis Visualizations and later she developed her own Bachian dance interpretations. She was a leading dancer during the Denishawn Asian tours, and then headed the faculty of Denishawn House in New York, in 1927.

After ten years at Denishawn, excelling in the Oriental and Music Visualization works, Doris felt that she had drawn from it all that she could. She was potentially a romantic dancer, perhaps of the Dionysian nature of Isadora. Her natural lyricism was heightened by the Denishawn training in the Delsarte principles.

Humphrey drew on the lore that had been accumulated for her at Denishawn, and from such parent sources she went out to explore further dimensions and evolve even more scientific theories for the dance of the twentieth century.

She had been a successful exponent of the Oriental styles. Still, she felt a nagging sense of longing to be more than a Denishawn dancer — more, even, than anything Doris Humphrey had yet been. But what was it that she truly wanted to *be*, and to *do*? To discover this Doris set herself a critical self-analysis. She found that while she knew many things, as for instance how the Eastern dancers moved, the one thing she did not know was herself and her own instinct toward dancing. *How would Doris Humphrey move in the dance if the dance were organic to Humphrey, as Music Visualizations sought to make dance organic to music?* It was a thought that startled and puzzled her, and then became the most important idea in her life. Isadora would have called it "inner voices," but Doris, skeptical of such supernatural persuasion, called it "inner and native rhythms." Whatever they were, she began to discover herself and her dance as though her body and the space around it were new, unsolved mysteries being revealed to her.

Doris Humphrey found herself in the looking glass. She stood before it and saw not Isis or an incarnation of legendary beauty, but Doris Humphrey herself. She was a tall, slender, graceful woman, fair, Titian-haired, with a face of patrician beauty. "She looked," as an observer noted, "like the child of the Morning Star." A great sense of strength and purity, of dedication, seemed to flow from Doris Humphrey the dancer. She had the "goddess" quality of great feminine beauty of face and form, and the serenity or inner authority that is the hallmark of the prima ballerina. But because she was a contemporary American, a child of the twentieth century, Doris Humphrey wished to dance the dance of her time and place.

Freeing herself of all she had learned, Doris waited for the creature in the mirror to inform her of Doris Humphrey's potential movement. Her tall, pliant body stood perfectly still, she scrupulously made her mind go blank and waited, merely breathing. Gradually, her body swayed and balanced in the natural but mysterious throb and flow of its life force. The *sway* carried past the point of balance became the beginning of a fall. With a conscious effort she regained balance and the fall was checked — she had recovered the original balance. Tempting a fall, she swayed farther, farther, and with the adjustment of her trained dancer's muscles she checked the fall. Abandoning this control, on the irresistible impulse to know what would follow, she fell, and made an involuntary effort to save herself. In so doing, she recognized a pattern of movement from the beginning of the fall, through her impulse to check it, into the finish of the fall, which was its accent. Then Doris noted that when she recovered her balance from a fall the movement had another pattern, a different accent.

She had made her personal discovery to create an evolutionary precept for Modern Dance.[40]

She described her theory with great simplicity: "My entire technique consists of the development of the process of falling away from and returning to equilibrium. . . . Falling and recovering is the very stuff of movement. . . . I recognized these emotional overtones . . . and instinctively responded very strongly to the exciting danger of the fall, the repose and peace of the recovery." But this theory and technique had two natures, one physical, the other psychical.

The simple process of *fall* and its natural corollary *re-*

covery contained three elements of dance. These were *design*, in the changing positions; *rhythms*, the accents that occurred at definite intervals; and *dynamics*, the varying degrees of tension. With these three Humphrey recognized a fourth and integral element, that of *drama* or emotion — the feeling experienced in the fall and in the recovery from the fall.

This was a brand new point of view for the dance, with motivation entirely different from that of the ballet aplomb.[41] In the classical theatre dance, where the defining characterization is architectural, aplomb, or equilibrium, is essential to line. Humphrey's theory had deep spiritual awareness and human compassion. She saw man's impulse toward progress, his ambitious drive, versus his desire for stability and peace as the excitement of movement and the exhilarating danger of fall. The balance and the recovery formed the peace of perfect equilibrium, of body and soul. Danger in the fall and repose and peace in the recovery reflected the impulse toward thrilling adventure and a yearning for peace. She believed that humanity exists in an area of spiritual conflict, exciting and dangerous, from which it alternately moves in an "arc between two deaths" — that of equilibrium or exalted quietude and the one of submission to an opposing force. She explained that "falling and recovering is . . . the constant flux which is going on in every living body . . . all the time."

This dramatic idea was the emotional source of Humphrey's work. She developed it organically, as a physical principle of dancing. She was extremely musical and she understood that within the movement of either *fall* or *recovery* she could design patterns out of rhythms, chiefly the regular rhythm of the body's pulse and the irregular, or uneven, rhythm of breathing. Exploration led her beyond the body into counterpoint. She designed dancing based on the contrasting rhythms of pulse and breathing to the accompaniment of yet a third rhythm, that of the music. She developed dancing without conventional music, as in *Water Study* (1928). For her famed *The Life of the Bee* in 1929, based on the Maeterlinck study, she used a vocal droning chorus. (It was later performed to Hindemith's Kammermusik No. 1, Opus 24, No. 1.) In 1956, her *Theatre Piece No. 2* was composed to sounds recorded on electronic tape, preceding by several years the Balanchine ballet *Electronics*.

The physical and the dramatic were as one and equally the basis for her work. "There is no gesture without meaning," she wrote, and she saw gesture as the visible extension of feeling. Gesture as stylized and formal as the handshake and gesture as passionate and sincere as the stamping foot and clenched hand were seen by Humphrey as "degrees of intensity of feeling." A gesture (the handshake) might begin from social usage and then appear in the dance, as the exact expression of the moment. So might the involuntary grimace or the wide-opened mouth, the wide-flung hand, signify an *intensified expression* in the dance. Joining the visual action and the spontaneous impulse as one, Doris Humphrey made gesture indistinguishable from movement for her dance. Her contribution to expressional dance and drama is one of the greatest ever made. In *The Book of the Dance*, Agnes de Mille says of Humphrey: "She is the only master ever to teach dance composition as a fine art in America."

Humphrey was a missionary of religious fervor possessed of a keenly analytical mind. Her approach to dance, her development of a new form and idea, and her work as choreographer and teacher had the crystal clarity of the diamond, and the illuminating fire. She loved humanity, but she had a ruthless sense of discipline for herself and for others. She believed with her whole heart that the intrinsic element of dance and the intrinsic quality of humanity were identical. She saw them as "purpose and will." From these came, muted or intensified, in shifting design, in regular and irregular rhythm, the drama that was itself the dance of life.[42]

The dynamic image that Doris Humphrey sought to communicate in dance was like that of William Blake (1757-1827), English artist and poet, a mystic who found mystery and beauty in life itself and believed that invisible spirit and corporeal body were fundamentally and indissolubly Man himself. Humphrey had the unshakable belief that Man's humanity was itself splendid and noble. Her repertoire was her testament to this belief, and her greatest single work is *New Dance Trilogy*, whose central piece is *With My Red Fires*, from Blake's *Jerusalem II*: "For the Divine Appearance is Brotherhood, but I am Love Elevate into the Region of Brotherhood with my red fires." Her sense of the divine quality of humanity and its dignity and power of endurance was personified in the monumental *Inquest*.

Doris Humphrey lived a strictly conventional personal existence. She was married in 1932 to a ship's officer named Charles Francis Woodford and was the mother of a son, Charles Humphrey Woodford, born in 1933. A woman of wide cultural tastes, she was stimulated by modern poetry, painting and music as well as by the dance. She received a Guggenheim Fellowship in 1949 for the writing of her book, *The Art of Making Dances*. Published posthumously, it now stands as one of the four great treatises on the subject. Since her career as dancer, choreographer and teacher was largely developed in the school and company she founded with a colleague, it must also be studied within the story of that colleague, Charles Weidman.

The foremost male dancer-choreographer of his era drifted into his destiny. Charles Weidman was born in Lincoln, Nebraska, in 1901, of English, Dutch and German antecedents. His father was a commercial illustrator, and young Charles inherited a flair for drawing vivid portraits from life. He was sharp and satiric, like a cartoonist. He used dance as his medium, and the stage for his drawing board. There Weidman sketched some of the most vivid characters and incidents of Modern Dance.

Charles had become hopelessly addicted to the theatre

from taking part in amateur theatricals during his school days. His father wished him to study commercial drawing, but Charles left home and made the long trek to Los Angeles and Denishawn. He joined the Ted Shawn Studio as a pupil, and there Shawn recognized Weidman's gift for characterization. It was one of Shawn's pet theories that there were two distinct approaches to dance, one masculine, the other feminine, and that these must be developed not only as characterizations but also in the technical training of the dancers, even in the music for the dance and the rhythms in the movements of dancing. Charles was a good student but he had no great self-confidence as a dancer. He was not shy and reserved like Martha Graham and Doris Humphrey, but he was so diffident that he lacked the dynamism necessary to the performer.

Shawn detected a flair for the comic in Charles and choreographed a comic dance for him, forcing him against his will to perform it. It was such a success that it gave Charles the self-confidence he had lacked, and a true delight in his power of antic mimicry. From then, he never looked back. He was a principal dancer at Denishawn and assisted Humphrey at Denishawn House in New York. When the school closed he joined Humphrey to found their own school and company.

They were joined by a third Denishawn member, Pauline Lawrence, and became known as "the Unholy Three." Pauline Lawrence was a high school girl in Los Angeles when she was asked to go to San Diego and play the piano as accompaniment for Shawn, then stationed at Kearny military base in World War I. One accompaniment led to another, and when Pauline left high school she slipped easily into Denishawn, where, like Horst, she was a pianist. When she joined Humphrey and Weidman she became a great deal more than a simple accompanist, because she was also publicity agent, costume designer and lighting expert. Graham had Louis Horst for her alter ego, and the Humphrey-Weidman company would not have developed to its fullest without the help of Pauline Lawrence. She was, in time, to be the indispensable aid of José Limón — and to become Mrs. José Limón.

"The Unholy Three" earned their title by their boldness in adventuring into the theatre with new ideas in dance and staging dance. The Humphrey-Weidman decor was revolutionary, as much by necessity as invention. It consisted of ten screens, 18 by 5 feet, with which they created wings, towers, and cyclorama, and which could also be turned into flats and double flats. Besides, they had cubes of quarter, half and double sizes which looked like children's giant "educational" blocks. These they used for stairs, castle ramparts, the steep slopes of mountains, or a plateau — even bushes or a sofa. With background draperies and skillful lighting, Pauline Lawrence transfigured the utilitarian props as though by magic, creating the correct atmospheres for the dance works.

Charles Weidman was a comic genius, inventive, fresh

and clever. His irony and satire were matchless. In his day, there was not an American man dancer to rival him as performer. His best moments were instinctive and he had the art of being able to transform personal experience into telling theatre. *On My Mother's Side* and *Daddy Was a Fireman* were semiautobiographical. His *Fables for Our Time*, from Thurber's writings, and *Flickers*, a parody on early movies, established him as a gifted comedian, but he showed yet another facet with *Quest* and *Atavisms*. In the latter, *Lynch Town* was so appallingly true to known events that it was an indictment of the era. Because Weidman was generally comic, his grave works had an anger and force that strengthened the sardonic, sometimes macabre dancing.

The Second World War interrupted Weidman's career. After serving in the U. S. Army he formed a company in New York and composed *A House Divided*, taking the role of Lincoln. In this work the Civil War was laid before the martyred President as if seen in retrospect after his assassination.

Weidman turned to the Bible for a work called *David and Goliath*, in which he altered the conventional characterizations and poked fun at the legendary pair. The dance was pseudo-archaic in style, and the characterizations were superbly and hilariously apt. Goliath was appropriately huge and colloquially "dumb," and David was a jaunty "boy wonder." The Philistines were a riotous and seedy mob, while the Israelites were well-behaved ladies who looked as though butter would not melt in their mouths. Weidman choreographed and danced everything he composed with fine style. He delighted in the witty and the wild, and had the reputation of "pulling the rug out" from under audiences, and of catching at their hearts just before they fell flat on their half-angry, half-mystified faces.

Like Humphrey, Weidman was intensely conscious of his fellow men. His pity and indignation over their wrongs were vented in sardonic comment or in a humorous pity, altogether unlike anything else composed for the Modern Dance repertoire.

He was apt to be overlooked between the feminine geniuses of Graham and Humphrey, but Weidman's value was incalculable to his theatre. He was a male dancer of imagination and skilled technique when such were rare in American dance. He had a masculine approach to dance at a time when a great deal of banality had crept into the theatre. When Charles Weidman simpered onstage it was with malice aforethought, with the use of the simper to make his telling point. He ornamented his profession with the bold color and impressive stripe of a tiger lily when it had become a poor joke to represent a *danseur* as a fellow who postured with a lily in his hand. Even at his playful best, Weidman had sinew and claw; he was more tiger than tiger lily as he pounced on human foolishness to make the audience laugh, or on an inhuman episode to shock the audience out of apathy.

"Packaged in Weidman's iridescent bubbles of dance," commented Margaret Lloyd, the celebrated critic of the *Christian Science Monitor*, "were kernels for rumination."

One of Weidman's most memorable works was his dance adaptation of Max Beerbohm's delightful fable *The Happy Hypocrite*. In the title role Weidman was Lord George Hell, a rake who assumed the identity of Lord George Heaven to woo an innocent country girl. In the mask of a handsome and uncorrupt lover he wins the lady's heart. The moral of the fable is aptly made when Lord George, falling in love in earnest, has his villainous heart altogether changed, and repents of his attempted seduction. When he tries to remove the mask he discovers that it has become his own true face, that he is no longer wicked Lord Hell but good Lord Heaven, and love has turned all his vices to virtues.

The dual role of Lord Hell and Lord Heaven gave Weidman an opportunity for showing his gift for mime, and his usage of masks was in the ancient tradition of the dance but brought to new and inventive style. His partner in *The Happy Hypocrite* was an exceptionally beautiful dancer of the Humphrey-Weidman company, Letitia Ide. This single work, in its excellence as dance and drama, won more response from the audience en masse than the whole repertoire of "gloom and doom" works had evoked for Modern Dance. It was one of the many works with which Weidman and Humphrey proved that the human principle inherent in Modern Dance could be accented rather than nullified by theatrical craftsmanship.

Weidman severely disciplined pantomimic gesture in the Modern Dance. His dance of itself assumed pantomimic qualities without affecting the dynamics of movement. Instead of the gross "expressional" gesture of older and more naive styles Weidman's dance united motives and rhythms as the whole dance phrase. He was especially forceful working with the dance of mimicry and satire, and his compositional patterns were original and of highly skilled structure.[43]

Unlike the dancers who took elegiac themes and legendary heroes for their inspiration, Weidman's materials were homely and familiar. His characters romped through circus and evangelical camp meeting with equal gusto. He drew from the Bible and the gymnasium. He did not hesitate to laugh at himself. On occasion, he poked fun at Modern Dance itself. Almost single-handedly this gifted comedian lifted his art to a high place at a time when the male dancer was still an oddity, and Modern Dance itself in danger of being engulfed in gloom and lost in mediocrity.

And Weidman, like Humphrey and Graham, had decided theatrical flair, the presence and dynamism to project to audiences. Theatrical spectacle is a highly skilled and ingenious craft and compositional dance (choreography for groups) a profession in itself. These skills enhanced the art of Graham, Humphrey and Weidman, who produced first-class theatre spectacles. It must be noted that theatrical spectacle and dance composition were important factors at Denishawn, and at a time when dancing was still in its ambiguous and naive soirée forms. The training and insight which Denishawn dancers received in their craft were significant in their presentations of the dance as art. And it was this professional authority in the theatre which established Humphrey and Weidman as the most distinguished partners of their era.

Doris Humphrey and Charles Weidman did not join the socialist dancers, and they did not seek to politically agitate the audiences for whom they danced. Instead, they worked in stagecraft with sincerity to present a repertoire that was handsomely mounted, costumed and danced. Many of their compositions had great substance and were serious in theme, but Weidman could not resist poking fun at some of his colleagues. In *Opus 51* he choreographed private jokes and personal caricatures that were recognizable both to dancers and general audiences. *Opus 51* caused a controversy between one faction who took it as an insult and another which delighted in this "ribbing" of Modern Dance, but it was one of the influences which restored the American contemporary dance to its original exuberance — the joyous rebellion rather than the propaganda tool.

Modern Dance now moved into higher education, into the United States college. Not so long before, it had been lifted out of the gutter by Denishawn. Humphrey and

Weidman joined the dance faculty at Bennington, while continuing to teach in their own New York school and to maintain a touring company. At first their students were only girls, but in 1936 Weidman began to teach a dozen male students. The enrollment grew with every year, and included not only physical education majors but students who were interested primarily in dancing as a career. A contemporary described them as "young people from all walks of life who were mad about dancing." The category of "young people" was strained to include teenagers and students who never admitted to more than thirty-nine. But it was true — they were all mad about dancing.

Graham, Holm, Humphrey and Weidman were known as "the Big Four" at Bennington, and their workshops produced the first major talents of the fourth generation of Modern Dance in America. They spent about a decade shaping the influence at Bennington, and these were years of wonderful vigor and experimentation for the dance in America. Meanwhile, the pioneer dancers were working and producing in the full strength of their artistic maturity. By the mid-thirties, Humphrey's work was recognized, and some of her compositions were being danced to full symphony orchestras in Philadelphia and New York.

Her first masterpiece was *Dance of the Chosen*, later renamed *The Shakers*, in 1931. Previously, her *Life of the Bee* had attracted attention of a serious kind for its merit as a dance composition. It also attracted general curiosity, because its accompaniment was nothing more than blowing through paper-covered combs. Humphrey's *The Shakers* was based on the worship of the Shaker sect, a religious group who were originally English Quakers and came to America in 1774. Their name was derived from the term "shaking Quakers" because of their habit of trembling violently in a sort of dance during worship; they believed that they manifested spiritual grace by such shivering and shaking. They were celibate, met in a meetinghouse for worship, and the men dressed in drab suits, the women in brown skirts and bodices and white bonnets. Humphrey faithfully followed all these details and choreographed a dance derived from the possessive, mystical fervor of the Shakers.

Never to be forgotten by those who saw her, Humphrey was the central dancer of the final movement. Here, with wide skirts swirling about her, Doris Humphrey lifted her arms, opened her hands, and raised a transfigured face. To the music of a drum, an accordion and a wordless soprano voice Humphrey and her dancers re-created a moment in the past for American theatre.

Because she was intellectual and analytical, Doris Humphrey made it a private fidelity to compose only what she knew or understood. Her *Dances for Women*, a modern fertility ritual, followed the birth of her child. She preferred composing works that involved other dancers to creating solos which would have exploited her gifts alone, and in 1935, making use of a large class at Bennington, she produced *New Dance*. It was the first full-scale work in Modern Dance, the first composition to extend beyond divertissement scale into large, symphonic structure. *New Dance* was a trilogy, of which the first two movements were *Theatre Piece* and *With My Red Fires*, which followed in 1936. (Weidman collaborated in *Theatre Piece*.) Altogether, this work was the largest for its style, and consumed a full evening in performance.

Following this monumental work, Humphrey composed some comedy pieces, one being *Race of Life*, drawn from Thurber's cartoons in *The New Yorker*. Other works were composed to Bach's music. Her *Song of the West: The Green Land, Desert Gods, and Mountain Rivers* was a loving salute to her native America. She might have rested on these, but she still had to compose *Inquest*, which would rival the fame of the *New Dance Trilogy*.

European observers of the American contemporary dance considered *Inquest* the single most profound work in American dance. "It is the dance," said a Frenchman, "which would cause the Bastille to fall again!"

Inquest is based on *Sesame and Lilies*, a verbatim account of a coroner's inquest into the death of an English cobbler in 1865, written by John Ruskin. The cobbler had died from overwork and starvation and the coroner said to the dead man's wife that it seemed deplorable to him that they did not go to the workhouse. The poor woman began to cry, murmuring that they wanted to keep their little comforts at home. What were the "comforts?" Weeping, the widow replied, "A quilt and other little things."

In 1865 Ruskin burned with indignation against the system of society that ignored such distress. He had his article printed in red ink. Humphrey, in 1945, felt the cobbler's sufferings as deeply as Ruskin, and composed a dance that scorched the stage. The cobbler and his family were portrayed with stark reality. A mass revolt erupted in the street outside the hovel as evidence of the wrath with which people responded to one man's death and one family's privation and despair.

Doris Humphrey danced the role of Mary Collins, the cobbler's wife, and was not seen as a dancer after that. Arthritis had gradually lamed her, and she would continue to suffer from that disease for the rest of her life. *Inquest* was not the last work she composed, although sometimes her slightest movement was torture. She could not walk without a cane and often leaned for support on another's arm, but she went on working as teacher and choreographer. She was the director of the Dance Department of the YM-YWHA in New York, and artistic director of the Juilliard Dance Theatre. She continued to travel in America from one school to another, visiting summer dance festivals, and even organizing new groups. She taught a repertoire of her works to the Juilliard Dance Theatre, a group emergent from the Juilliard School of Music; sponsored the Merry-Go-Rounders, a group of adults specializing in dances for children; and was on the advisory panel of the International Exchange

Program of the American National Theatre and Academy (ANTA). Doris Humphrey by the 1950s was acknowledged from every quarter for her creative genius and the influence and leadership she personified for Modern Dance.

Some of her best work was composed for José Limón, in *Lament for Ignacio Sanchez Mejias, Day on Earth, Ritmo Jondo* and *Ruins and Visions*. The dance was an intensely personal thing for her, as it was to all the pioneer Modern dancers, but she choreographed with as much power of invention and truth for other dancers as she would have for herself.

Humphrey was the most direct, lucid and analytical of the pioneers, and she was the one most understanding of the audience. She saw that public acceptance of Modern Dance was necessary if the dance was to survive and grow. She refused to believe that Modern Dance was either a precious art for the intelligentsia or for "the masses," or that the tastes of any coteries should decide the state of the dance. Like a strong, invigorating wind, the Humphrey-Weidman company cut a path between the controversies. They refused to be catalogued with the "gloom and doom" dancers, and they had no intention of restricting their repertoire to themes admired by left-wing groups. Humphrey accepted the fact that Modern Dance was new and strange to the general audience, and she would not make it so lofty or esoteric that it would be incomprehensible. She said of her work that she wished her dance to be based on "reality illuminated by imagination; to be organic rather than synthetic" and that she wished to make her dance a contribution to the drama of life.

The Humphrey-Weidman influence extended from the classrooms where they taught to the general audience in American theatre. They conducted dance demonstrations to interest the uninformed audience and to explain the styles and principles of the contemporary dance. Their tours in the United States, the New York concerts, and dance festival and workshop appearances were largely instrumental in keeping Modern Dance alive and growing during its most difficult years. Humphrey preferred to work at home, believing that the contemporary dance needed to become known and treasured in America. As a result, she was known to foreign audiences only by repute, from the reports of visitors to the United States, and through her influence on the work of José Limón. She was the more articulate of the Humphrey-Weidman school and freely expressed the principles taught there.

Her system of teaching was the most clear cut and meticulous of her time. She disliked "artiness" and evasive outlines in dance. Other dancers might need to commune with the Muse, she commented, but for herself she wished to communicate with dancers in the rehearsal studio and the audiences in the theatre. To her students she spoke in the most practical terms. The hands, she said, were the most expressive parts of the body, and the most sensitive. She saw the hand as the root human gesture in the drama of life. The back of the hand was negation and dismissal. The hand palm upward, up and out, extended or curved, could hold, comfort, soothe, give and receive. She saw the palm of the hand as "a beneficence" and reminded her dancers that for centuries all peoples had used the human hand to express offering, greeting, tenderness, compassion. For every gesture she asked: *What does it mean?*

Her intent was clear to her audience. "I wish to call forth definite reactions," she said. Therefore, she never despised the audience, or danced "down" to it or thought of herself as dancing "up" to cliques. She danced *because* of a purpose, with a will toward communicating and awakening response. A pedagogue, she was positive and definite, but she was not pretentious. And she produced the most exciting and provocative dancer of the next era, Sybil Shearer. Shearer wrote that she went to study with Humphrey because here was a teacher who was not dogmatic; she worked for quality, she urged her students to, above all, *dance.*

Pauline Koner is the dancer who best evokes the image of Humphrey and qualifies the precepts Humphrey advocated for dance in its spiritual concept and its art of performance. A remarkable empathy existed between these two women, who were unlike each other and highly individualistic. Humphrey was not, in the strictest sense, Koner's teacher, for Koner was already established as an artist of stature, and on an international scale, before she worked with Humphrey.

A child prodigy in dance, Koner is wholly unique. She

is not descended from any branch of the Modern Dance's "family tree." She was the student of Fokine, the Spanish dancer Angel Cansino, and the Japanese dancer Michio Ito. She danced in Fokine's company when she was fourteen, then in the companies of Michio Ito and Yeichi Nimura, and from 1931 traveled extensively. In Russia, she was warmly welcomed as a Fokine protégée. In the 1940s she returned to America. She is the wife of the conductor Fritz Mahler.

Koner's association with Humphrey began with the younger dancer's interpretation of the Mother in Humphrey's *Ruins and Visions* and lasted until Humphrey's death. Koner was the partner of José Limón in his company, helping him to create some of the masterworks of Modern Dance, like *The Moor's Pavane*, Limón's epic translation in dance of Shakespeare's *Othello, the Moor of Venice*. She was the principal feminine member of the Limón company until 1960, when she returned to solo work within her own company. In 1962 Koner composed *The Farewell*, a tribute to Humphrey. That and a later solo, *Solitary Song*, marked the flowering of Koner's genius. Her phrasing is original (dancing based on a key movement or a series of key movements from which other movements perfectly and naturally unfold) and in 1964 she received the Dance Magazine Award for "a unique sense of perfection" in the art of performing. Her celebrated teaching course, "The Elements of Performance," embodies the principles of Humphrey's theoretical concepts for dance arts. Koner has said of her mentor, "Since her death, she inhabits me. She is my *dybbuk*." (A *dybbuk* in Jewish folklore is the soul of a dead person who rules the body of a living one.) The affinity between the two dancers is twofold. Humphrey advocated dance performance as theatre and Koner's dancing is itself a masterpiece of technique and magnetism, which she teaches as *focus* and *dynamics*. And Koner's testament for dance is exactly akin to that of Humphrey, who before her death told Koner, "We [the dancers] must not forget nor let the audience forget the wonder of the human spirit."

José Limón is Humphrey's most famous pupil and protégé. Katherine Litz is the one of the women she taught who most resembles her, not in imitation but in the same feminine approach to dance. Her pupil Shearer is the possessor of a troubling gift, an inspired lunacy. There are several Humphrey-Weidman pupils performing and teaching in the present era. One of these, Eleanor King (head of the Dance Department of the University of Arkansas), materially advanced ethnic dance in Modern modes. The relationships between primitive ritual and the form generally called "Modern" represents one whole aspect of the contemporary dance. The sources have been imported, as from the African (Pearl Primus and Percy Borde) or Jewish (Hadassah), as well as indigenous, as in the use Eleanor King has made of American Indian ritual and regalia in her dance works.

The Humphrey-Weidman techniques are brilliant theories in Modern Dance. Humphrey's philosophy of dance was in the concept that humanity is essentially noble, not vile. She was motivated by the sense of spiritual dignity and divinely granted human will, and the consciousness of the materialistic world. Weidman was a comic genius, but his collaboration with Humphrey was so harmonious that while they were both distinctive and original dancers, each assumed some characteristics of the other. Humphrey was sometimes satirical, and Weidman, especially in his later works, showed a gentleness and sense of classicism reminiscent of Humphrey.

Now in his sixties, Weidman remains active as a dancer, choreographer and teacher with a troupe of his own. He maintains a New York studio, frequently performs in New York concerts, and is well known in the American university dance for his lecture-demonstrations and dance workshops. He has contributed uniquely to the dance appreciation of this era's audiences by his loving interpretations of some of his famous contemporaries. An unparalleled stylist in Modern Dance, Weidman has been able to evoke for audiences today the characteristic fleetness of Harald Kreutzberg and the spirituality of Humphrey. He is an exceedingly important link between two epochs.

Hanya Holm

In order to appreciate the contributions made to the American Modern Dance by Hanya Holm it is necessary to trace her roots to the German dance. Hanya Eckert was born in Worms, in the first decade of the century. Her father was a prosperous wine merchant from a family of Bavarian brewers, and her mother, primarily a housewife, was also a scientist and chemist whose family was seriously interested in the arts. Some relatives were professional actors.

Hanya Eckert attended a convent "progressive school" of the type which rapidly advanced the avant-garde principles of twentieth-century educators. Students were tutored in small groups, under strict discipline, but with equal emphasis on science and art. From this formative environment Hanya drew a feeling for perfectionism and an understanding of the interrelation of science and art, significant qualities in her work as a choreographer.

She studied the piano from the age of ten and at sixteen graduated from her convent, going into the Dalcroze Institutes at Frankfort and Hellerau to continue her musical education. At twenty she married a painter-sculptor whom she subsequently divorced. She had one child, Klaus Holm.

As a child she had been strongly affected by Pavlova's performances and she had wished to study ballet with the intent of becoming a professional dancer. Her father disapproved of dance as a career for his daughter, who turned instead to one in music. But when she saw Wigman she was again strongly moved toward dancing. Coincidentally with her divorce she began to study dance, which soon absorbed her to the exclusion of all other interests. She has said that, to her, the dance is so absorbing that it is impossible for the dance artist to devote himself to any other thing, or to another person. Deeply reserved by nature, she found that dancing demanded of her an extraordinary effort, and preferred composing to performing. But, after a period of study under Wigman, Holm became a member of Wigman's touring group. She appeared in Max Reinhardt's production of *The Miracle*, (a notable event in the theatre of that era) and danced a leading role in Stravinsky's *L'Histoire du Soldat*. And she was a dancer as well as a technical assistant in Wigman's antiwar memorial pageant *Totenmal* (*Death Monument*) in Munich.

She became increasingly interested in teaching dance and showed such talent for this that Wigman made her director and chief instructor of her Central Institute in Germany. Wigman danced in America in 1930, 1931 and 1932 and in 1931 sent Holm to New York to teach the Wigman principles of dance in an accredited school.

Holm thus found her most creative forte. Her idea of teaching was more than the bare system of instructing. For her, dance meant using the analysis of self within a technique of movement. She believed that the teacher must open new vistas for the student. The ideal communication between student and teacher lay within the roots from which they stemmed, and the knowledge to extend beyond the known and the familiar. The process of teaching, for Holm, was one of perpetual growth, exactly as for the process of learning. She said: "Whatever I know, I learned through teaching."

While almost every other major dancer was working in passionate zealousness to express a personal philosophy in dance, Holm began to work in her New York school with precise and almost rigid regard for the Wigman principles. Gradually she saw that Wigman's dance's total nature was systematic and insular, indeed Germanic, while that of the American Modern Dance was already eclectic in time and place, and of its very nature free and adventurous. But she also saw that a great deal of the American dance was derived from personalities, and so conclusively on these that a basis of instruction was needed to maintain a standard of performance. Holm's dance was based, in its Germanic ideas, on physical and cosmic laws, but Holm herself was sensitive to the personality of the individual dancer.

She adapted the Germanic dance to the particular American characteristics of the dancers she taught in her new country, breaking part of the tie which bound her to Wigman while securing herself within the American Modern Dance tradition.

The graft of German dance which Holm succeeded in making brought a new vigor as well as a new discipline into the American mode. Her sense of drama as being intrinsic to the movement of the dance was a characteristic of her work. She had an economy of gesture and a sharp sense of objectivity. Her concert performances in the college theatre advanced the admirable rapport the Humphrey-Weidman group had begun with the general audience.

Her greatest aesthetic contribution to the American Modern Dance was in the use of space. The "birdlike swoop" of the Holm dancer became a hallmark of the teacher. She used Wigman's scientific theories for teaching dance but with her own understanding of the American dancer's physical and metaphysical attributes. Her dance form of "spatial command" is based on centrifugal and centripetal forces and on other natural spatial laws. Her system propounds movements diagrammed in curves, verticals, horizontals, to which the dancer individually relates, physically and emotionally. These were theories essential to the German dance as expounded by Laban and Wigman, but Holm's ability to invest them with an American character gave them the distinction of "Holm lyricism." [44]

In 1936 her New York school was reestablished as the Holm School, and she joined the faculty at Bennington College Summer School. Since 1937 she has directed summer courses in dance at Colorado College. Her most celebrated pupil is Valerie Bettis, who was the first Modern dancer to compose works for traditional ballet companies (*Virginia Sampler*, 1947, and *A Streetcar Named Desire*, 1952). Other famed Holm students are Mary Anthony, Eve Gentry and Glen Tetley, and she has guided Bambi Linn, Rod Alexander, Uta Hagen and Zachary Solov.

Holm's greatest work was *Trends*, a heroic dance-drama in which she performed in 1937. The critic John Martin, who for years set the only printed accolades on the Modern Dance, hailed it as the greatest composition of that year and described it as blazing a trail for a greater synthesis of all the arts. Holm extended her work into the musical theatre. She is the choreographer of the Broadway musicals *Kiss Me Kate*, *My Fair Lady* and *Camelot*. She directed the opera *The Ballad of Baby Doe*, and her *Metropolitan Daily*, a satire on newspapers, was the first Modern Dance composition to be televised by the National Broadcasting Company. She has worked in the popular theatre as choreographer, director and producer. But Holm's greatest and most far-reaching influences are not in the theatre pieces she has choreographed. They lie in the notable teachers of her system, Holm students who direct dance instruction in major colleges in the United States. These include Francisco Boas, Shorter College; Nancy Brock, Purdue University; Shirley Dodge, University of Texas; Bruce King, Adelphi College and Columbia University; Louise Kloepper, University of Wisconsin; Millie Lynn, Bennington College; Martha Coleman Myers, Smith College; Elizabeth Waters, University of New Mexico; and Martha Wilcox, Denver University. Holm is also the teacher of Alwin Nikolais, a noted teacher and choreographer.

✍ *Tamiris*

The contemporary dance is poetically described as "a divine indiscipline" because its spirit is impulsive, its nature free. Its growth and development resemble nothing so much as a living tree, spreading its branches and sometimes intertwining them, up from the main stems and roots. The lineage or "family tree" of the American Modern dancers is peculiarly like a human one, swarming with relatives-by-blood and relatives-by-marriage. Influences are directly derived from teacher to student, or in flashes of inspiration from outside forces, like Pauline Koner. Holm was a graft, an imported German influence which adapted to American dance while influencing it. And there were independent shoots who were not directly attached either to Denishawn or to Wigman, but grew and flourished in other climates, from other sources. One such, and a wild, sweet branch, was Tamiris.[45]

Born in 1905, she inherited the theatre that others, like the Denishawn Company dancers, had made for her generation. When Tamiris was growing up there were several places where even the poorest and most underprivileged American child could study dancing, although there was nothing like the large scale and official patronage of dance which other leading nations have long advocated. No state, civic or federal grant was given to the humanities and fine arts in America. But other grants began to be awarded to American dance. Among these were the Guggenheim and Rosenwald awards. Foundations like that of Elizabeth Sprague Coolidge and the Alice M. Ditson Fund at Columbia University encouraged dance artists. New York was in the van of this patronage, and one of the oldest and best-known concert theatres for contemporary dance was created on Lexington Avenue and Ninety-second Street in the YM-YWHA — the Young Men's and Young Women's Hebrew Association.

Modern Dance entered schools and colleges in America through physical education, and its forms became widely used as physical exercise and group movement. Other countries, particularly the Scandinavian nations, included gymnastics in normal education, and Dalcroze Eurhythmics and Delsarte's principles accelerated the development of dance within physical education. American educators adapted these so advantageously that not only schools but also settlement houses included dance in curricular activities. One settlement house was established in Chicago by Jane Addams, and the Henry Street Playhouse in New York came into being in 1915 under two sisters, Alice and Irene Lewisohn. Irene Lewisohn studied Delsartian movement under Genevieve Stebbins, and was influenced by Oriental dance and the plastique mode. She inaugurated a dance education, of which Tamiris was a product.

Helen Becker, who later became known as the dancer Tamiris, was from a Russian-Jewish immigrant family of remarkable character. The Beckers were poor and lived in a tenement district in New York, but one of Tamiris's brothers was a painter, the other a musician and sculptor, and their father and mother had an Old World sense of family solidarity and individual responsibility. Helen Becker was a very pretty child, with bright blue eyes, red curly hair, and a tremendous vitality. She attacked life with such gusto and self-confidence that one of her child-hood associates remembers her as creating about herself a perpetual whirlwind of argument. To keep her off the streets of the brawling district where they lived, the Becker parents sent their little daughter to the Henry Street settlement house, where she danced for exercise and recreation.

The child's enormous nervous energy was soon directed into a craze for dancing. Her family had bundled her off to the settlement house to save her from being run over, or worse, on the streets, but they were dismayed that the Lewisohn influence was urging Helen on to the stage. Mr. Becker wanted her to have a college education and he insisted that she finish high school. On graduation, at fifteen, Helen applied for a dance audition at the Metropolitan Opera House. She turned up in gym tunic and bare feet, with hair flying, just as she was used to dancing at the Playhouse, and found that the other candidates were correctly dressed in ballet clothes. "Guess I'm in the wrong place!" she muttered. But the ballet mistress, the ballerina Rosina Galli, told her to stay. Helen did and won an award which gave her three months' ballet lessons without charge, a job thereafter at twelve dollars a week, and free training at the Metropolitan Ballet School. She was later a student of Fokine, became a ballerina and toured South America with the Bracale Opera Company.

But she was not satisfied with the ballet and moved into jazz, performing in New York musical revues and supper clubs. Still she was dissatisfied, as she was with every style of dance which had already been exploited. She saved enough money to give herself a year and a half to work and study alone, and in search of her dance style she assumed a new identity as "Tamiris." She chose her name from a poem about a Persian queen: "Thou art Tamiris, the ruthless queen who banishes all obstacles." When she was ready, she appeared in her new character in a New York concert.

American Modern Dance had taken on some of the grimmest hues of the German dance, and Tamiris exploded like a vivid flash of color on the scene. Because she was very pretty some critics refused to take her work seriously. She went to Europe and was an instantaneous success. She was the first American, after Duncan, to be invited to dance at the Salzburg Festival. Europeans were as much affected by Tamiris's beauty as they had been by Duncan's and St. Denis's, and she attracted artists and intellectuals as the older American dancers had done in their time. On her return home, Tamiris took her place in the forefront of Modern Dance. She organized a Dance Repertory Theatre, hoping to gather into one group all the leading Modern dancers. She hoped to integrate the principles and influences of major and revolutionary artists, of Graham, Humphrey, Weidman, and Agnes de Mille, and to join hers to theirs. Of these, de Mille was an unclassifiable dancer, using styles that ranged from the free Modern forms to the ethnic dance, mingling folk dance with ballet. In 1943, de Mille changed the course of American musical theatre through her choreography for *Oklahoma!* by making the dance organic to the drama. Thereafter, dance in musical revues began to develop its own artistic standard to match that of dance in the opera and concert theatre. Several ballet and Modern dancers followed de Mille's lead, Tamiris among them.

Tamiris did not succeed in maintaining her Dance Repertory Theatre and she was not one of the Bennington group. She worked by herself and then in collaboration with her husband, Daniel Nagrin, an exceptional dancer who was also a choreographer. Nagrin had a brilliant technique that did not obscure his magnetic physical attraction, and he complimented Tamiris, who had a warm and richly colored beauty. Tamiris is the bacchante or maenad of the American contemporary dance, closest in type to Isadora.

Tamiris is well known to the general audience as the choreographer of the musicals *Annie Get Your Gun, Inside U. S. A.* and *Plain and Fancy,* in which Nagrin created important roles. She danced and choreographed for the American Dance Festival at New London, Connecticut, and had a company, The Helen Tamiris-Daniel Nagrin Company, in which her husband was codirector and principal dancer. Nagrin later toured as a lecturer and soloist.

Like a wild branch, Tamiris grew vigorously, and with her physical beauty and an especially flowing grace of movement she added a feminine sweetness to the starkly realistic Modern Dance. Her repertoire falls into two categories: one for the concert theatre, the other for musicals. Her major concert works include *How Long Brethren,* to Negro songs of protest; *Liberty Song,* based on Revolutionary songs: "Bunker Hill," "Ode to the Fourth of July," and others; *Adelante,* inspired by the suffering of the Spanish Civil War; and *Cycle of Unrest,* inspired by her preoccupation with social injustice.

Artistically she was an innovator in her use of accompaniment for dance. *Triangle* presented Tamiris and three girls with triangles which they played while dancing; a solo, *Lull,* was danced to cymbals. Her work was characterized by a fierce sincerity and a passionate awareness of the individual. All the Modern dancers were shouts to the world, each declaring the "I" and calling out to be heard. In *The Individual and the Mass* and *Dance of War,* Tamiris uttered her doctrine: a personal dignity, and sensitivity to injustice and cruelty. In her *Walt Whitman Suite* and others she reiterated her pride in her native land. Whether on the concert stage or in musical revues, Tamiris the choreographer was essentially American in creativity. She used American themes with love and theatrical insight, and her repertoire eloquently expresses the American spirit through representative regions and types.

Younger than the other pioneers, she inherited a wider theatrical domain. Tamiris, like her contemporary Anna Sokolow, was among the rich little poor children in America who made good use of the wealth of education spread before them. These two, Tamiris and Sokolow, emerged from settlement house dance training. Others, like Esther Junger, came from physical educational dance in American schools.[46]

❧ IV ❧

A Summation

WE KNOW the rebellions and reforms which developed Modern Dance, but it is not easy to categorize Modern Dance today. The dance itself is a living force, *a dynamic image dependent on the living dancer*. As such, it is never static, and although a style may be re-created from a past period, the dancer in his own time defies arbitrary analysis and definition. Perspective alone grants sufficient critical insight to fully estimate the dancer and his dance. But at mid-century there were certain aspects of the American Modern Dance which qualified its new theories and compositions.

Modern Dance began with the urgent demand to express. It was a state of mind before it became a way of movement. Now contemporary dancers prefer to discard feeling as motive and theme and allow the dance to exist for movement alone. The young American dancers are investigating ideas in movement instead of the expression of the inner self in dance. They are reflective of a new philosophy. The new dance is not yet concise except as a dance of technical innovations, the dance as move-

ment for source and content — an end to its own beginning as abstract movement, nonobjective except in the
tension between the physical movement itself and its
existence in the dancer's mind.

This approach to dance has appreciably dissolved the
original barrier between ballet and Modern Dance. This
is the epoch of the choreographer, and the dance's aesthetic substance is absolutely determined by its great
choreographers. Major evolutions in dance have come
from Merce Cunningham, a Modern dancer, and from
George Balanchine, whose training and tradition is ballet.
These are two creators of abstract dance.

Graham and her contemporaries created techniques
through which to express themes and characterizations
that were then unusual to the ballet. Fantasy and poetry
were common to the romantic ballet. Delicacy, buoy-
ancy, line and symmetrical aplomb are ballet's characteristics in movement. The pioneer Modern dancers
preferred to invent a dance vocabulary that was less of
the theatre and more of the street. They were impelled
by strong emotions, some of them violently in conflict
with society, which they communicated in an idiom more
appropriate to its themes. Thus they created movements
that broke altogether with ballet's scrupulous definition
of technique. As modern composers made music on new
chromatic scales far removed from the diatonic scale and
older harmonic structures, so the Modern dancers discarded ballet's five positions and turn-out and accepted
the flexible qualities of the human body as the dance

source. Duncan made her impulse the solar plexus. The new concept of movement allowed an invention of dance idiom which spanned the human emotions and their physical impetus.

Beyond this epoch of the dance (which came to its burgeoning before mid-century) there was another artistic revolt and one as controversial as any recorded in the arts. It has served to unite artists of certain convictions whose first traditions were divided between the ballet and Modern Dance. James Waring was a *danseur* of the ballet. Merce Cunningham and Erick Hawkins had been Graham's partners and had created notable roles in her dramatic repertoire. These three are to be classified not only as being of the ballet or as Modern dancers but, more conclusively, as being among the American abstract dancers. They are commonly referred to as avant-garde.[47]

The clearest means of perceiving the new revolt is to compare it with previous rebellions and the reforms which emerged from them. To relegate all abstract dance to the "avant-garde" confuses the dance of tomorrow with the dance of yesterday, since "today" is yesterday's tomorrow and tomorrow's yesterday. But we possess a "new" dance in the same way as we have a new generation.

Aspects of the era's social behavior and philosophic thought have included the "beat" and derivations of Zen Buddhism. They are, in part, indicative of free response to mood and moment, as differing from a philosophy dependent on logic. In music, the composer has now moved beyond all conventional form in the use of natural and mechanical sounds, which some composers manipulate in the way that the surrealist and collage artist manipulate materials in painting or sculpture.

Two contemporary French composers, Pierre Barbaud and Roger Blanchard, have utilized a mechanical calculator, Binary Digital Computer Gamma 3, which mathematically "composes" music as it would an abstruse mathematical equation. This is within the theory (existent since the seventeenth century) that music is an arithmetic process carried to its logical and absolute limit. Influenced largely by Arnold Schönberg, such composers create in the twelve-tone scale. The abstract choreographers who recognize the relationship between music and mathematics, between pure science and art, have adopted what they consider a logical evolution for dance. Their concern is with structure and the substance of dance. Reality exists not in plot and characterization but in the choreographer's mind and the process of creation. Other composers and choreographers of avant-garde music and dance speculate on the intuitive potential of chance. Haydn relied heavily on the laws of probability and sometimes rolled dice to make his choices between possible chord and key combinations. On the theory of "indeterminate" or chance creativity composers like John Cage and choreographers like Merce Cunningham have developed aleatory forms of music and dance. Indeterminate or aleatory music draws its meaning from the Latin *alea:* a game of dice.

The avant-garde composer resorts to unconventional means for producing his music. Cage has a "prepared" piano and his contemporary, Harry Parch, invents his own instruments for performing his music. Many composers compile "musical scores" by creating sounds and combining them with natural or mechanical sounds (rain and a metronome; ocean waves and a clacking typewriter) which they record on magnetic tape. Such tape registers more minute distinctions of pitch and variations of tone than conventional musical instruments are capable of doing, when played by human musicians. Inspired by the radical composers, dancers of avant-garde theories take modern music as their point of departure for the dance. Some choreographers compose in silence and after completion of the dance engage a composer to invent a musical score, thus establishing two separate artistic creations within a single work. Other choreographers compose through a method of numbers, an arithmetic device, and in strictly geometrical patterns with or without manual use of props from fabric or other materials. There is a school of thought, and a technique of dance, by which certain choreographers develop their dance as "discovery." One such choreographer is Alwin Nikolais, who defines his device as metaphorical, and declares himself as abstracting from normal gesture (of ordinary persons in familiar or everyday functions) a "direct kinetic statement." Such a device separates functional movement from the movement emerging out of emotion. Like pure music, which is "heartless" or devoid of conventional feeling, the abstract dance is pure dance.

The young choreographers are positive and articulate. They fluently translate their dance into description and statements of aesthetics. But they are concerned primarily with dance, and it is within this form of personal expressiveness that they communicate with audiences. Modern Dance has never ceased to intrigue the audience, but its contemporary form makes increasing demands on the audience's appreciation, and in this aspect it — with a great deal of the "abstract" ballet — has come to be thought of as "cerebral" dance.

The broad basis for a serious appreciation of Modern Dance comes from the American educational curriculum, especially that of college dance courses and college theatre. And the veriest "average" member of the general audience may grasp the technical and aesthetic recognition of "the dance of today" by letting it assume the factors of contemporary painting and music. The new American Modern Dance propounds several theories common to other contemporary arts. It is possible to trace into the dance some of the same imagery and artistic impulse that characterized Joyce and Eliot.

In "choreography by chance" a reversal or a distortion of a natural movement (a dance "action" normally made frontwards executed sideways or backwards), and acceleration or slowed-down timing of movement, makes extraordinary what is in itself ordinary. These dance "actions" are queerly alien. In a literary connotation, the dance is like a poem in a new meter, in which the stress appears always to fall on the unexpected word.

Stillness has become an aesthetic phase of the abstract dance, as silence was a phase of Wigman's early dance. Paul Taylor is Cunningham's contemporary and, like Cunningham, a dancer of astonishing technical accomplishments and revolutionary theories. They have strongly influenced the United States college dance and have caused sensational demonstrations abroad for and against the new American abstract dance. Taylor is a painter as well as a dancer and expresses his choreographic intent in line. He thinks of movement as a painted line and sees it as making a direct, pictorial statement or a shapeless (and meaningless) scribble. He may, for a dance, combine the elements of both types of "line" so that a walk or a run by a dancer erupts into wild, vague gestures. Taylor has carried the stillness in abstract dance to its apogee in *Duet*, in which a couple at a cocktail party stand stock-still for four minutes. It is an abstraction in dance comparable to Kasimir Malevich's painting *White on White*, a "picture" visible only to the eye perceptive to its abstract qualities.

Cunningham and Taylor, who choreograph and dance in their own companies, have revolted from dance in which the drama is endemic. Because they emerged from the Graham company their rebellion is particularly obvious. As Graham has become increasingly literal, the younger dancers have become arbitrarily abstract. The argument which the new Modern Dance makes is that movement alone is the subject of dance.

In this, they return in some measure to the principles for ballet, which center on movement and a stylized technique for the performance of movement. The ballet choreographer makes multiples of movements, like pirouettes, and invents complicated combinations of movements, and exciting and unusual juxtapositions of the combinations with qualitative timing and accent. The action of balancing, in any of ballet's five positions, might be construed as an exercise in stillness in the dance. And the ballet artiste performs *terre à terre* and *en l'air*, adagio and allegro. While the ballet choreographer used only music of the older forms his ballets had a character like the music: elegant, gracious, virtuoso. But many modern ballet choreographers have turned to the most revolutionary concept of music, with resulting "modernistic" impetus on ballet. Ballet may now be totally abstract in precisely the aesthetic sense of the "new" abstraction in Modern Dance, while remaining, within its form and technique, classifiable as seventeenth-century theatre dance.[48]

The Modern Dance does remain wholly individual in its movement sources, directions and statements. It is still the "barefoot dance" and although many Modern Dance works are sumptuously set, on the whole its costuming is still functional, with a strangely antique classicism, a sculptural quality accented by fabric and lighting.

The new Modern Dance choreographers treat movement like matter, finding interest in shapes and textures. They require the audience to accept the experience of the dance as valid, and they maintain that one perception immediately leads to the next. They employ some of the techniques of the abstract painter whose picture of seemingly incongruous lines and colors and disconnected masses does not depict a concrete object but purely and intimately associates the subject of the picture in the vital "experience" it provides.[49] The new Modern dancers still see their dance as "a dance of experience."

This "experience" is encountered by the American audience in a variety of theatres, some of the salon and soirée character not too far removed from those of Isadora's time. The ballet in America has been centered in major companies of which there were three in mid-century: the Ballet Russe de Monte Carlo (presently disbanded), the American Ballet Theatre, and the New York City Ballet. The average theatregoer could see any or all of these and make a fair estimate of ballet in America. There are also regional ballet companies ranging from the national renown of Chicago's Opera Ballet under Ruth Page and San Francisco's ballet company under the Christensen brothers, to amateur and semiprofessional groups.

Modern Dance has not been brought to the average theatregoer on any such scale. There are one or two major companies, of which Graham's and Limón's are unequaled and the most permanent. And there are innu-

merable groups and troupes of varying size, production
and repertorial scope and status as permanent and active
"companies." Festivals like the annual ones at Connecticut College, Jacob's Pillow, and Idyllwild, California,
bring together Modern dancers within separate groups
and as soloists. But despite its undisputed place as art
dance, Modern Dance is still disorganized and controversial. Much of it is amateurish and mountebank in theatrical presentation as dance.

Modern Dance is disorganized because the great creative artists still remain autonomous. Their pupils, protégés and "disciples" are generally intolerant of all other
systems of training. In this respect, the individual Modern Dance "systems" are now far more iconoclastic than
the ballet. The more fervent a pupil of a great Modern
dancer, the more chauvinistic and insular.

The controversies within Modern Dance are largely re-
sponsible for the controversies about it. The average
theatregoer has no concept of the distinctions of the creative process. It is these very distinctions which have
made, for instance, "Graham dance" issue from Martha
Graham, while another dance issued from Humphrey
and Weidman, and a third from Holm. The abstract
Modern Dance accepts the technical vocabulary of the
pioneer dancers while rejecting their motivations. It was
a change in ideas, not in idiom, which affected the dance
at mid-century.

All choreographers are dancers, but in the ballet every
great dancer is not necessarily a choreographer. In Mod-

ern Dance, almost every major choreographer is also a noted dancer. The very genius of such dancers isolates one from the others of his kind. Tamiris made a laudable effort, but failed to organize her peers. Modern Dance lacks an authoritarian guide. It has never had an unprejudiced, critical guide and mentor and many argue that if it ever does it will be at the loss of its special character.

This special character derived from its rebellion, and yet a great deal of what Modern Dance revolted against has been reformed, and according to Modern Dance's ideals. It was primarily a romantic revolt, but Modern Dance has passed through phases which have moved it far from romanticism. It sought perceptual image of the inner self, but it has since rejected feeling (which some dancers now call ephemeral sensation) as well as narrative and continuity. Denigrating the principles of the dramatic dance, it has developed an abstraction which, as it creates its own dogma, may come to contain as much as or more symbolism than Graham's dance. Modern Dance has a character of constant inconstancy. It is the dance of life, like life itself.

The altercations over aesthetic philosophies and forms, over the dancers' motivations and styles, bewilder the audience en masse. Yet Modern Dance has never been more alive and vigorous than it is now, especially in the United States colleges.

Liberal arts colleges in the United States have played an important part in nourishing the Modern Dance. Following the lead of the University of Wisconsin several colleges offered dance degrees, some in physical education, others in fine arts. These included Mills, Bennington, and Sarah Lawrence colleges. By the 1940s dance was a major subject in the curriculum and a normal part of physical education in high schools as well as in colleges. Educators saw the dance as contributing in education to total health and fitness, as self-expression, and as an excellent group involvement for the individual. The dance, said psychologists, offered a means of self-expression and creativeness and a valuable philosophy of play.

The first real progress in dance education was made through teachers colleges, where instructors like Louise Bayliss at New York University and Mary O'Donnell at Columbia taught high school teachers how to move from formal school gymnastics into the principles of Modern Dance training. Following the introduction of such flexible dance techniques into the normal school curriculum came folk and social (ballroom) forms, and the wealth of music and drama educational facilities that are now the common perquisites of American schools.

In 1935 the dance project of the Federal Theatre, subsidized by the Work Progress Administration (WPA) to help solve unemployment in the theatre, was active in New York and Chicago. It included ballet but was primarily for Modern Dance assistance. And in this decade Modern Dance began to assume a system and terminology, while the ballet began to borrow some of Modern Dance's free style and expressiveness. Jooss spent little time in America, but his theory became representative of the American twentieth-century dance — chiefly, that *Modern Dance better expresses the human state of our century than the classical seventeenth-century ballet, but the maximum expressiveness and interpretation come from both the classical and contemporary styles of dance.*

The American dancer now has unlimited freedom to create. He ranges in the theatre from musicals to opera, and he is no longer a rebel and a social outcast. Besides the serious consideration the audience grants him, he now has earned the respect of his government. The State Department's cultural exchange programs regularly include dancing for export to foreign theatres. The astonishing novelty of this condition for the dancer in our society today may only be realized by comparing it with that of Duncan's time, and the times that Duncan changed for herself and her successors.

The work of the choreographer and the dancer is now accepted as possessing the same merit and eloquence as those of the poet, painter and composer. It is possible that history will place the American Modern dancer in the highest rank among his contemporary artists, for it is this dancer who has been the great revolutionary, the most original and inventive in his art.

Appendix

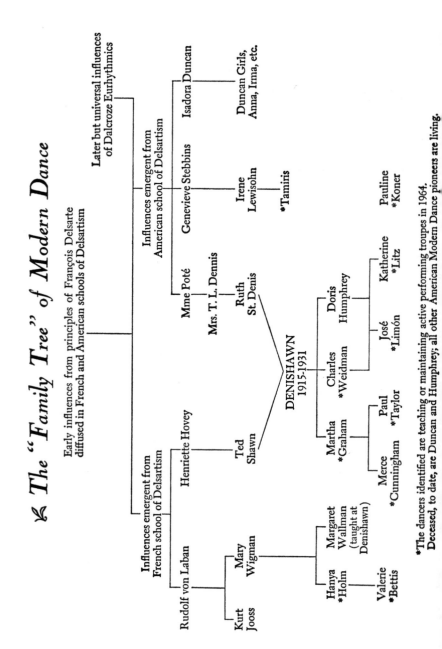

The "Family Tree" of Modern Dance

Early influences from principles of François Delsarte
diffused in French and American schools of Delsartism

Later but universal influences
of Dalcroze Eurhythmics

Influences emergent from French school of Delsartism

Influences emergent from American school of Delsartism

Rudolf von Laban

Mary Wigman

Henriette Hovey

Mme Poté
Mrs. T. L. Dennis

Genevieve Stebbins

Isadora Duncan

Kurt Jooss

Hanya *Holm

Margaret Wallman
(taught at Denishawn)

Ted Shawn

Ruth St. Denis

Irene Lewisohn

*Tamiris

Duncan Girls,
Anna, Irma, etc.

Valerie *Bettis

DENISHAWN
1915–1931

Martha *Graham

Charles *Weidman

Doris Humphrey

Merce *Cunningham

Paul *Taylor

José *Limón

Katherine *Litz

Pauline *Koner

*The dancers identified are teaching or maintaining active performing troupes in 1964.
Deceased, to date, are Duncan and Humphrey; all other American Modern Dance pioneers are living.

⧉ Notes

1. Among the best literary sources for ballet's technical form is *The Classic Ballet*, by Lincoln Kirstein, Muriel Stuart and Carlus Dyer, Alfred A. Knopf, Inc. Others are *An Elementary Treatise Upon the Theory and Practice of the Art of Dancing*, by Carlo Blasis, and *Fundamentals of the Classic Dance*, by Agrippina Vaganova, Kamin Dance Books, New York. In addition, several books on ballet contain glossaries with line drawings of the technique, such as *Balanchine's Complete Stories of the Great Ballets*, edited by Francis Mason, Doubleday & Co., Inc., and Olga Maynard's *The Ballet Companion*, Macrae Smith Co.

2. Ballet's earliest academic base was in a room in the Louvre, where in 1661 Louis XIV established a school under thirteen dancing masters. Louis XIV was an accomplished *danseur* from childhood, and his famous title *Le Roi Soleil* (The Sun King) came from a role he danced in a ballet. The seventeenth-century French Académie Royale de Danse has endured through intervening centuries into the present Paris Opéra ballet school and is the oldest ballet school in the world. Ballet was developed in the Renaissance, and early in the 1400s a codi-

fied form existed. The codified form for the ballet we know today dates from the 1600s. The first ballet of this form was presented in 1580 by an Italian violinist and dancing master, Balthazar de Beaujoyeulx, at the court of Catherine de Medici, an early patroness of the dance and a balletomane who infected her descendants with her admiration.

3. The formal structure of Modern Dance in its elements of dynamism, metakinesis, substance and form was analyzed in the 1930s. There are several literary descriptions of these elements, the most lucid being *The Modern Dance,* by J. J. Martin, A. S. Barnes & Co., Inc., 1936. Other excellent sources for literary descriptions of the dance and dancers' styles are contained in *The Dance Encyclopedia,* by Anatole Chujoy, A. S. Barnes & Co. Inc.; *A Dictionary of Ballet,* by G. B. L. Wilson, Penguin Books Ltd.; and *Modern Dance Terminology,* by Paul Love, Kamin Dance Books.

4. The science of archaeology is comparatively new. Until 1875, when it was granted full status as a separate and distinct science, it had been treated as a part of philology. Then, it became part of the general field of the humanities and its intellectual stimulus was immediate and immense. The first half of the twentieth century is designated "the archaeological age" because of the activity of archaeologists from several countries and the vast amount of information their finds yielded to civilization. One of the most exciting finds was made in 1900 by the Englishman Sir Arthur John Evans, who at Cnossus unearthed an unknown Minoan civilization. A German amateur, Heinrich Schliemann, made amazing discoveries, start-

ing as early as 1875, of the sites of Mycenae, Troy and Tiryns. Greek and Roman civilizations exerted enormous appeal for artists, and a neoclassical age in art emerged from the science of archaeology. It had effects on painting and dance, described in the chapter on Isadora Duncan.

5. Sigmund Freud (1856-1939) was an Austrian psychiatrist and the originator of psychoanalysis, the minute examination of the mind to discover the causes of behavior. Freud endeavored to explain the human unconscious's "normal" or natural behavior and its relationships in art, religion, mythology, folklore, dreams, language, and wit and humor. Although he was ridiculed and his theories have remained controversial, psychosomatic medicine is in large part the result of his early work. He lectured in the United States in 1909.

6. Friedrich Froebel (1782-1852) was so far in advance of his time as an educator that he was persecuted in Switzerland and Prussia. A Prussian edict in 1852 forbade the establishment of schools on the principles he advocated. The basis of his theories for educating children was early training in a suitable environment, like that of the kindergarten, developing mind and body through voluntary activity. His *Chief Writings on Education* appeared in English in 1932 translated by S. S. F. Fletcher and J. Welton.

7. The development of the "psychological" novel is paralleled in the famous Tudor ballets, psychological dance dramas which are compared with the writings of D. H. Lawrence. Tudor is also compared to Guy de Maupas-

sant and the composer Richard Wagner. Descriptions of his choreographic works are in the biography of Antony Tudor, in Olga Maynard's *The American Ballet*, Macrae Smith Co., pp. 127-138. Agnes de Mille, Eugene Loring and Jerome Robbins are American choreographers who used Modern techniques with classical, folk, and even jazz forms of dance to create memorable works. They, too, often made the formal structure of the dance emerge organically from the human characterization and dramatic plot or incident. Examples are de Mille's *Rodeo*, *Fall River Legend* and *The Harvest According*; Loring's *Billy the Kid*, *City Portrait* and *Prairie*; Robbins's *The Cage*, *Facsimile* and *The Age of Anxiety*. For these also, see *The American Ballet*.

8. The main characteristics of nineteenth-century music were feeling and imagination, "tone-painting" and virtuoso elegance and brilliance. These yielded to Impressionism, Expressionism, polytonality, atonality, and functionalism. Claude Debussy, the friend of Impressionist painters and symbolist poets, was greatly influenced by the radical composer Erik Satie. Debussy shunned everything rhetorical and fervent. He turned music from its human or emotional element toward what modern composers consider an exemplary objectivity, and thus he marked a new musical era. His revolutionary harmonies were the beginning of a new musical language. After him Arnold Schönberg, Alban Berg, Richard Strauss, Béla Bartók and Igor Stravinsky made significant contributions to that language. Jean Cocteau described the musical change: "After music with the silken brush, music with the axe." Similar revolutionary changes took place in the dance, and not only between ballet and

Modern Dance. In the latter style, the romantic and lyrical modes of Duncan and Ruth St. Denis yielded abruptly to the angular and percussive forms of Mary Wigman and Martha Graham. And in the twentieth century music assumed immense importance within the dance, sometimes to the eclipse of drama and of feeling in the emotional sense. George Balanchine in ballet and Merce Cunningham in Modern Dance are choreographers whose works show a total regard for music, and sometimes for music of the most avant-garde nature. Balanchine's *Electronics* is performed to electronic sounds taped as a "musical score." Cunningham's collaboration with the American composer John Cage provides several other examples. Cage's "indeterminate music" sometimes consists of rattles, bangs, pops and nonsense syllables roared at tremendous volume into microphones, augmented by piano duets and the whirring of an electric food blender. His *Music Walk With Dancer*, 1962, has been called an electronic nightmare. The twentieth-century musical departures from poetic feeling and composition provoke thought rather than emotion and have been designated "cerebral music" in the same way that some styles of dance are classified as "cerebral ballets." Such dance is the antithesis of ancient dance, for which music did not exist as "pure" music of itself but was performed for the express purpose of dance accompaniment.

9. The "madmen" of music and "wild beasts" of painting were artists of radical influences who helped to change twentieth-century art. The orthodox techniques and subject matter of the conservatory and academy displeased them as much as the theatre dance dissatisfied Isadora

Duncan. Like Duncan, they gravitated to Paris, the center of rebellions and reforms. Here the Spanish painter Pablo Picasso became the genius of modern painting, while the Russian composer Igor Stravinsky became the giant of modern music. But first came the century's early scandals and the quarrels over the madmen and the wild beasts.

Erik Satie (1866-1925) was an eccentric and original composer who influenced *Les Six*, the composers Georges Auric, Louis Durey, Arthur Honegger, Darius Milhaud, Francis Poulenc and Germain Tailleferre, four of whom are front rank contemporary composers. They admired Satie and were renegades against the pedagogic, as exemplified by the works of Vincent d'Indy (1851-1931), whose principles of teaching were based on the Gregorian chant. Some of them were attracted to American jazz. But it must not be thought that an organized and cohesive reform took place in music. The Six did not agree as a group, especially about Wagner, whom Honegger admired and Milhaud despised. The individuality and dissention in musical rebellions were comparable to those in Modern Dance.

Les Fauves, the "wild beasts" of painting, were André Derain, Othon Friesz, Henri-Charles Manguin, Albert Marquet, Georges Rouault, Jean Puy, Louis Valtat, Cornelius Van Dongen, and Maurice de Vlaminck, and their leader Henri Matisse. In 1905 an art critic, Louis Vauxcelles, saw an exhibition in which a work of Donatello's seemed to him, in juxtaposition with modern paintings, to be placed among "wild beasts," forms so savage and alien that they were beyond art. A furious quarrel raged through successive waves or schools of painting between artists and their critics and, very often, between artists of one school and another. And here again the Modern Dance has a history very like that of modern painting.

10. Delsarte's Laws, and the Modern Dance's primary applications of them, are described in *Every Little Movement*, by Ted Shawn (published by the author). It was originally printed in 1954 and reissued in a new edition in 1963, and is an invaluable one-volume study of Delsartian principles. It contains charts based on Alfred Giraudet's important source book on Delsarte. Delsarte called Giraudet his finest disciple. Shawn was a pupil of Henriette Hovey, who studied in France under Gustave Delsarte, the master's son.

11. Marie Rambert, born in Warsaw in 1888, went to Paris in 1906 to study medicine. She had studied dance and gave private dance concerts in Paris, where she soon discovered her interests to lie wholly with the theatre. Much influenced by Duncan, she began to study with Dalcroze from 1910 and later taught in his Dresden school. Serge Diaghilev and Vaslav Nijinsky, in the process of setting *Sacre du Printemps*, asked her to assist with the complicated rhythms. She joined Diaghilev's company, where she became a pupil of Enrico Cecchetti. Settling in London, she studied under a celebrated Russian teacher, Serafina Astafieva, married an Englishman and opened a school in 1920. From 1930 she presented ballets at the Mercury, owned by her husband, Ashley Dukes. The Rambert Ballet is the oldest active ballet company in Great Britain. Rambert was created D.B.E. for her contribution to Britain's national arts. She is the subject of a brilliant pen portrait in *Dance to the Piper* by Agnes de

Mille, Atlantic–Little, Brown & Co. *Rambert, Dancers of Mercury*, by Mary Clarke, A. & C. Black Ltd., London, is a definitive biography.

12. Laban's principles were developed on a geometric form, the icosahedron, a twenty-sided solid figure. His theories for dance "swings" contributed to primary spatial developments for the dance, and are based on the continuous, weaving line of the figure 8. His system, Labanotation, is taught through an American Dance Notation Bureau in New York. An exponent of the system, Hildegard Blum, is the author of A *Primer for Dance Notation*.

13. Kurt Jooss took the third step in logic and system for the dance, still in the directions set by Delsarte and Laban. Jooss's development was Eukinetics, and he divided movement into outgoing and incoming within divisions he called central and peripheral. His great ballet was *The Green Table*, 1932, whose topic and characterizations aroused a great deal of discussion. Its theme is satirical. Politicians meet over the green table to decide the fate of helpless peoples. Jooss brought a company to the United States and made world tours. He lived and taught in England during the war and returned to Essen, Germany, in 1951.

14. Harald Kreutzberg was an exceptionally handsome dancer whose personality was a great theatrical asset. He considered the substance of Modern Dance to lie, entirely, within its aspect of "a definite stylistic phenomenon, analogous to the appearance of expressionism in painting." In this relationship, the expressionistic dance is like Expressionism in painting, for example, the works

of the German Max Beckmann. It was more characteristic of the German dance than of the American.

15. *Prometheus Bound*, the subject of Aeschylus's play and
    Shelley's poetic drama, is one of Shawn's best known
    solos. He created it in 1929 to Alexander Scriabin's
    Poème Tragique, setting the dance on a narrow ledge
    against a rock to simulate the bleak promontory on which
    the angry gods chained the fire-stealer. With his right
    ankle and left wrist bound to the rock Shawn's dance
    movement was limited to the reach of his chains. It was
    his purpose to show the dance as "a study in limitation
    — triumphant." In theme the messianic rejoicing of Pro-
    metheus (who obtained fire for mankind and was pun-
    ished by the Olympian gods for stealing it) exalted the
    physical limitations of the dance. In costume, Shawn's
    Prometheus Bound and his *Death of Adonis,* another
    solo work, set precedents for the male dancer that were
    even more revolutionary than Duncan's for feminine
    dancers. Shawn danced *Prometheus Bound* in a loin
    cloth, and, *circa* 1920, as Adonis, wore the classical fig-
    leaf and white body make-up to give the effect of a
    marble statue. Shawn and St. Denis were sticklers for
    authentic effects, and this passion for verisimilitude had
    unforeseen results when Shawn, wreathed in fresh forest
    greenery as the god Pan, discovered, too late, that he had
    been decked in poison ivy. According to Shawn (see
    Shawn, *One Thousand and One Night Stands,* Double-
    day & Co., Inc., 1960), *Death of Adonis* was the first
    plastic dance. "Plastique" was a much used and abused
    term for a style in Modern Dance. It was properly used
    to differentiate dance of the "new" mode from the
    ballet, which emphasized the linear and silhouette as-

pects of the nineteenth-century theatre dance. Modern
Dance was concerned with the body as mass and substance, and its full powers of expression and physical
plasticity.

16. Loie Fuller was the daughter of an itinerant fiddler, born
on a very cold winter's night in a barroom, the only place
in Fullersburg, Illinois, with a stove. As an infant, she
leaped onstage during a revival meeting and recited
Mary Had a Little Lamb. Hauled off by her embarrassed
mother, Loie returned to the stage before she was in her
teens. She was a seasoned trouper when she, by accident,
discovered the charm of a skirt dance. She had trouped
all over the United States and as far as England, where
she doubtless had seen versions of the "skirt dance" innovated by a popular music-hall artist, Kate Vaughan.
Fuller was looking through a trunk for a costume to wear
in a new show when she came on a filmy, voluminous
skirt of silk gauze. The light from a window shining
through the fabric seemed to illuminate it. It gave her
her first insight into the values of light in the theatre.
Later, she wore a costume that was so long it almost
tripped her. Holding it up, while dancing, she found that
the drapery added a great deal of effect to her dance.
Thereafter, Fuller, cleverly costumed and lighted, set a
vogue for dances in which she seemed a butterfly, a
flower, a fairy of light. She went to Europe following an
unhappy love affair with the nephew of Rutherford B.
Hayes and was soon the star of her own show. She made
friends with important people, among them the scientists
Pierre and Marie Curie and the astronomer Camille
Flammarion, who instructed Fuller in the physiological
and psychological determinants of color on plants and

humans. She was intimately associated with the great, and was an artist of worth in her epoch. One of the most famed mementoes of her is Toulouse-Lautrec's lithograph, of which the artist made only fifty, which he colored by hand and powdered with gold dust. Ballets and music-hall acts copied her work, dancing à la Loie Fuller. This extraordinary American woman, pug-nosed and said to look like the twin sister of Oscar Wilde, invented a mixture of fluorescent salts and paint, which she put on her glowing skirts and stage draperies. Her inventions resulted in the "cold" light for theatres, whose commercial uses include markings for air raid shelters. Her scientific discoveries far outclassed her talent for dancing. Two of her famous solos were *Fire Dance* and *Serpentine*. Born in 1862 or 1870, Fuller died of pneumonia in 1928. Her contributions to the modern theatre rank with those of Gordon Craig and Adolph Appia, who were chiefly concerned with stage decoration on an architectural scale. She was naively unconscious of the worth of her discoveries and experiments with lighting, many of which were precedents for the modern theatre. Her autobiography, *Quinze Ans de ma Vie* (1908), had a foreword by Anatole France.

Maud Allan came from an environment different from Fuller's and Duncan's. She was beautiful, well-educated and a trained pianist. For her dancing she adopted Neo-Grecian styles of classical draperies and bare feet and used the music of great classical composers as accompaniment. Her most famous work was *The Vision of Salomé*. Her friend, the composer Marcel Remy, worked in close collaboration with her, arranging and composing music for her dances. Allan had a good reception when she danced in New York in 1910 although she, like Isadora, danced in a state of undress far from the conventional mores. Allan died in California in 1956, aged seventy-three. She wrote several articles on the dance and an autobiography, *My Life and Dancing* (1908).

Contemporary U.S. writers on the dance barely acknowledged these two women. A true gauge of their values in theatre may be gleaned only from the reviews and essays written about them within their lifetimes. It is of note that Fuller commissioned an original musical score and produced a version of the biblical Salome's story with her own choreography at the Théâtre des Arts, Paris, in 1907. Serge Diaghilev used this same music for his production of *La Tragédie de Salomé* in 1913, with choreography by Boris Romanov. It was Isadora chiefly, but not Isadora alone, who influenced ballet and art dance early in the twentieth century.

17. The Empire and Alhambra theatres were the centers of English ballet, and the frankly commercial contest between them heightened the British audience's appreciation of dance. At the Empire the exquisite Danish ballerina Adeline Genée appeared in works ranging from the puerile to the artistic. *Around The World Again*, *The Milliner Duchess* and *High Jinks* appealed to the audience en masse, but that same audience was beguiled into seeing *Coppelia*, *Sylvia* and *Giselle*. The Alhambra's repertoire boasted ballets called *The Handy Man* and *A Day Off* but it imported notable dancers, many from the Russian Imperial Ballet. Ballet was seriously, even opulently, treated in Russia under the patronage of the czarist court, while in the Western nations it was being viewed as frivolous or immoral. But since the schools maintained an explicit regime for training dancers, the

ballet survived its theatrical decadence. This was the era
of the ballerina, as the twentieth century became the era
of the choreographer. Many of the ballets were merely
vehicles for the more spectacular accomplishments of
their stars. It is necessary to know the conditions and
public opinions which influenced the theatre dance of
Europe, Britain and America in order to understand the
purposes and results of Duncan's rebellion against ballet.
American ballet prior to the twentieth century is briefly
described in Maynard, *The American Ballet*, Macrae
Smith Co., pp. 15-33, "The Beginnings." British ballet
is well chronicled, and may be researched in the work
of contemporary writers like George Bernard Shaw, who
wrote theatre criticism during the heyday of Empire and
Alhambra ballet. Modern writers like Ivor Guest have
added to the record with books and monographs on the
period dance and dancers.

13. Botticelli's *La Primavera* (Springtime) hangs in the Uffizi
Gallery in Florence. It is sometimes called *The Allegory
of Spring*. It depicts Venus in a garden of orange trees
laden with golden fruit, strolling with her nymphs on
green grass studded with flowers. At Venus's side Flora,
the goddess of flowers, strews the ground with blossoms
carried in the skirt of her flowered dress. On one side
there is a group of dancing nymphs and on the other a
wind-god clasps a terrified nymph, freezing the flower
between her lips with his icy breath. Reproductions of the
famous painting appear in innumerable art books, two of
these being *Botticelli*, a biography by Elizabeth Ripley,
J. B. Lippincott Co., and *A Treasury of Art Masterpieces*, edited by Thomas Craven, Simon & Schuster, Inc.

19. Terra-cotta figurines dating back to the fourth century B.C. were discovered at the excavations in Tanagra, an ancient Greek town on the Asopus River. The Tanagra figurines are graceful statuettes, painted and gilded, representing everyday people. The Greeks used them as household ornaments and as deities in ceremonial religious offerings. They became a fount of inspiration to painters and dancers of the twentieth century.

20. The Five Principles of Michel Fokine, on which he based his reformation of the classical ballet, were published in *The Times* of London, June 6, 1914. They are paraphrased in several books on ballet, one being A *Dictionary of Ballet*, G. B. L. Wilson, Penguin Books Ltd.

21. An article on the relationship between Isadora Duncan and Constantin Stanislavsky, based on his book and letters recently released in Russia, appeared in *Dance Magazine*, July 1963.

22. The "impulse" of which Duncan spoke and wrote has been misinterpreted by contemporary writers, teachers and dancers to mean that Isadora's dance was naive improvisation, movement without plan or purpose that sprang from the impulse of the moment. This is altogether untrue. Isadora Duncan's impulse or source was her serious précis for a new dance movement, and it was immensely important and significant. It is to be traced into the works of all major Modern dancers, under various terms, as is shown in the chapters and notes relevant to these pioneers. Isadora's search for a "new" dance was austere and profound. She said: "For hours I would stand quite still, my two hands folded between my breasts,

covering the solar plexus. I was seeking and finally discovered the central spring of all movement, the crater of motor power, the unity from which all diversities of movement are born."

The Duncan "impulse" and source for dance was new, and different from that of the ballet. Nineteenth-century ballet treated the dancer's trunk or torso as an erect column, and the arms and legs, especially the legs, were animated by dexterous and difficult combinations of movements. "Feats of dance activity" for the spectacular nineteenth-century ballet resulted in remarkable contortions. (See Olga Maynard, *The American Ballet*, Macrae Smith Co., p. 25, "The Beginning.") Duncan wrote that "the ballet schools taught the pupils that this spring [the central point within the body from which all movement springs] was found in the center of the back at the base of the spine. From this axis arms, legs and trunk must move freely, giving the result of an articulated puppet." Duncan's principles for a "new" dance literally broke the erect, rigid back of the ballet dancer, which thereafter assumed the plasticity which is a marked characteristic of the twentieth-century ballet.

23. The Diaghilev era, 1909-1929, brought about "modern ballet," in technique and ideal largely based on Fokine's principles. A concise account is given in A *Dictionary of Ballet*, under Diaghileff, which is especially useful in following the evolutions in ballet music and costume and design. Much of this was contributed by composers and painters of note, like Stravinsky and Picasso.

24. Duncan wrote two books, *My Life* (1927) and *The Art of the Dance*, published posthumously (1928). She is the

subject of many books and essays, some of criticism and others of a sentimental nature like *The Untold Story* (1929), by her friend Mary Desti. The most authoritative study, to date, is *Isadora: A Revolutionary in Art and Love* (1960), by Allan Ross Macdougall, Thomas Nelson & Sons. The most recent biography is *Isadora Duncan, Her Life, Her Art, Her Legacy* (spring, 1964), by Walter Terry, Dodd, Mead & Co. *The Technique of Isadora Duncan* by Irma Duncan Rogers is a text for dance instruction and describes the dance based on natural movements, walking, running, skipping, jumping and the swingstep, with correlated arm positions somewhat similar to ballet's *port de bras*. Besides the "general rules" for performing the Duncan style of dance, this manual offers lessons in the waltz and the polka and for the "Tanagra Figures." Duncan's death anniversary date invariably produces material on her life and art, especially in periodicals like *Dance Magazine, Dance News, Dance Observer* and *Dance Perspective*, the last specializing in monographs. The best literary observations of dancers are made by their contemporaries. Carl Van Vechten, American critic, made important literary contributions to the dance from the 1900s. Contemporary writing on Duncan, and on Fuller and Allan, appear in *Dancing and Dancers of Today* (1912), by Caroline and Charles H. Caffin, Dodd, Mead & Co., and *Modern Dancing and Dancers* (1912), by J. E. C. Flitch, J. B. Lippincott Co. *Chronicles of the American Dance*, edited by Paul Magriel (1948), Henry Holt & Co., Inc., is a collection of contemporary studies. The most intimately experienced and vividly described rapport between Isadora Duncan and her audiences is by Margherita Duncan:

"The first time I ever saw Isadora Duncan she was dancing on the Carnegie Hall stage to the music of Gluck's *Iphigenia*. I experienced what I can only describe as an identification of myself with her. It seemed as if I were dancing up there myself. This was not an intellectual process, a critical perception that she was supremely right in every movement she made; just a sense that in watching her I found release for my own impulses of expression; the emotions aroused in me by the music saw themselves translated into visibility. Her response to the music was so true and inevitable, so free from personal eccentricity or caprice, her self-abandonment to the emotion implicit in the music so complete that although I had never seen nor imagined such dancing, I looked at it with a sort of delighted recognition. I think this experience of mine must have been common among her audiences; for the desire for beauty lies at the bottom of every human heart and she gave it expression, so that in watching her we had a sense of satisfied longing."

25. *An Unfinished Life*, by Ruth St. Denis, 1939, Harper & Brothers, New York.

26. For some understanding of the nineteenth-century ballet in America, in the "candlelight and gaslight" era, see books and photographs dealing with the theatre of Anna Held and Lillian Russell, Tony Pastor and burlesque "idols" such as "Little Egypt." A brief but bright view is to be seized from *Can Can Americana*, by Harold Meyers, 1951, Avon Publishing Co. Inc., and in the chapter "The Beginning," in Olga Maynard's *The American Ballet*, Macrae Smith Co.

27. Modern Dance in Germany pretentiously assumed the titles "dance with a purpose" and "art dance," to distinguish it from the dance as puerile or "popular" entertainment. In America the terms never came into common usage. Mary Wigman called her work "New Dance."

28. Mrs. Dennis's grasp of theatre essentials was truly astonishing in a woman without professional training. An anecdote shows her flair and the extent of her influence over St. Denis's work. On a European tour with her daughter, Mrs. Dennis was recalled home to nurse her ailing husband. She left "Buzz" (alternately known as "Brother" St. Denis) to watch over Ruth, who was composing *The Nautch*. Ruth composed no less than seventeen versions of this dance, but she, "Buzz," and the distracted theatre manager could not decide on *the one Nautch*. Summoned to Paris by cable, Mrs. Dennis arrived and sat down, still wearing her hat, to view all seventeen versions of *Nautch*. Then Mrs. Dennis, with the air of choosing one puppy from a litter, picked her choice of *Nautch* and drowned the rest. *Nautch*, incidently, was premiered as advertised and was one of St. Denis's major successes.

29. *One Thousand and One Night Stands*, with Gray Poole, was published by Doubleday & Co., Inc., 1960. Shawn is the author of numerous articles and essays, and his books to date are: *Ruth St. Denis: Pioneer and Prophet* (1920), *The American Ballet* (1926), *Gods Who Dance* (1929), *Fundamentals of a Dance Education* (1937), *Dance We Must* (1940; 4th ed., 1963), *How Beautiful Upon*

the Mountain (1943), *Every Little Movement* (1954; 2nd ed., revised, 1963), *33 Years of American Dance* (1959), *The Story of Jacob's Pillow* (1962), and a music publication, *16 Dances in 16 Rhythms* (1956). *The Seven Magic Years* (1963), edited by Joseph E. Marks from the correspondence of Shawn and Lucien Price, editor emeritus of the Boston *Globe*, relates the touring years of Shawn's Men Dancers. *Shawn, The Dancer* (1933), by Katherine S. Dreier, is a biographical study with photographs and text for Shawn's solo and group choreography. A *Biographical Study of Ted Shawn; His Life, Professional Career, and His Influences on Dance* is the doctorate paper of Betty Poindexter, Texas Woman's University (1963). A *Chronology of the Professional Appearances of the American Dancers Ruth St. Denis and Ted Shawn, 1906-1932,* is the doctorate paper of Christina L. Schlundt, University of California at Riverside. The Schlundt *Chronology* was published by the New York Public Library in its monthly bulletins and was reissued in book form by the Library in 1962.

30. See Shawn, *One Thousand and One Night Stands,* Doubleday & Co., Inc., 1960.

31. The Denishawn Music Visualization theories predated the specific Dalcroze method at Denishawn, which was later taught in the school by Elsa Findlay. In 1925 St. Denis wrote a description of her inspiration and working principles for Music Visualizations, and claimed to have coined the phrase Music Visualization to avoid the much-abused word "interpretive" as applied to dancing. She related that one experience in particular, a dancer performing to

the music of a large symphony orchestra, led her to the analysis and resolving of fundamental truths about the relation of dance and music. St. Denis's essay on this theme appeared in 1925 in *The Denishawn Magazine*, a publication of her school and company. These magazines are now collector's items but are still accessible in many public libraries in the United States.

Modern Dance has claimed the principle of "music visualization" as one of its great innovations, but ballet repertoire abounds with examples of the same theory and principle, notably in Michel Fokine's *Les Sylphides* for the Diaghilev ballet in 1909 (it was originally *Chopiniana* in Russia, from a 1907 production by Fokine, and it remains under this name in Soviet ballet repertoire, and for some European ballet companies who mount versions of *Les Sylphides*). This is a ballet of pure mood, without plot. It is accepted as the precedent of ballets where the dance is pure interpretation of the music in terms of movement. It is the forerunner of the symphonic ballet which was developed by Fokine, Bronislava Nijinska, Leonide Massine and George Balanchine, and of which Massine's *Les Présages* (1933), set to Tchaikovsky's Fifth Symphony, is the first of the genre. "Symphonic ballet" came into vogue in the 1930s when Modern Dance's "music visualization" was falling from favor. Dancers, among them Doris Humphrey, became convinced that music "visualization" (dance as purely interpretive movement of music) was inadequate, because music does not operate spatially in the same sense that the dance does. Music Visualization, per se, was abandoned by Modern dancers whose theories were that movement was the substance of dance. These dancers believed that the dance was independent of music and could possess form and character of itself as an art. (See the chapters on Wigman and the Americans Humphrey and Graham, and principles of "absolute dance" on page 25.) In tracing Modern Dance's "music visualization" and the ballet's symphonic form to their roots we come to Isadora Duncan's influences — she danced to Beethoven's Seventh Symphony, creating a furor, which was, incidentally, re-created in New York in the 1930s over Massine's usage of classical symphonic compositions for his ballets, *Les Présages, Choreartium, Symphonie Fantastique* and *Seventh Symphony.* These were composed to music by Tchaikovsky, Brahms, Berlioz and Beethoven. And, before Isadora, Beethoven's Fifth inspired other dancers. It was a feature of the ballet *The White Fawn* at Niblo's Garden in New York in 1868.

32. See Katherine S. Dreier, *Shawn, The Dancer,* A. S. Barnes & Co., Inc., 1933.

33. See Christina L. Schlundt, A *Chronology of the Professional Appearances of the American Dancers Ruth St. Denis and Ted Shawn, 1906-1932,* New York Public Library, 1962.

34. Louis Horst was an eminent musicologist, author of *Pre-Classic Dance Forms* and *Modern Dance Forms,* and editor of an important publication, *Dance Observer,* which he founded in 1934. During his liftetime he was titular head of contemporary dancers, and the closest thing to their accepted authority. Shortly before his death he was awarded a Doctor of Humanities degree.

Agnes de Mille drew a vivid portrait of him in *Dance to the Piper*, and *Dance Magazine*, in its issues from January through April 1953, described his life work.

35. However, Graham categorically states (to this writer) that she was not influenced by jazz, per se, and that her work, *Frenetic Rhythms*, is not based on jazz although critical writers have arbitrarily determined that it is.

36. From Agnes de Mille, *Dance to the Piper*, Atlantic–Little, Brown & Co., 1952.

37. "Contraction-release" is one of the main principles of Graham's dance, others being "motor memory" and percussive movement. Graham says: "I use the term 'release' to express or denote the moment when the body is in breath, has inhaled, and has an aerial quality, and the term 'contraction' when the drive has gone down and out, when the breath is out." Graham evolved a system of floor exercises, which she describes:

"The first movement is based upon the body in two acts of breathing — inhaling and exhaling — developing it from actual breathing experience to the muscular activity independent of the actual act of breathing. These two acts, when performed muscularly only, are called 're-lease,' which corresponds to the body in inhalation, and 'contraction,' which corresponds to exhalation."

38. The English ballet developed a national tradition in the twentieth century, only a few years before one was developed in the United States. Despite the influences of Marie Rambert, British ballet remained almost wholly in the character of the Russian Imperial Ballet. Rambert pro-

duced the first original choreographic genius in British dance, Antony Tudor, but he worked in America from 1939, and none of his ballets have been produced by Britain's national company, the Royal Ballet. Graham in 1963 was said to have received the greatest acclaim ever accorded a dancer in London. Following this success, dancers of the Royal Ballet took classes from Graham, and Graham's pupil Yuriko taught classes to students of the Arts Educational Trust, an English vocational school.

39. The dance work protested was *Phaedra*, Graham's treatment of the heroine of a tragedy which Euripides, Racine and others have interpreted. On September 9, 1963, Brooklyn Congresswoman Edna F. Kelly and New Jersey Representative Peter J. Frelinghuysen told a House foreign affairs subcommittee that they had been so shocked by *Phaedra* that they had been forced to walk out during its performance in Cologne, Germany, in 1962. Graham had included *Phaedra* in her repertoire for a tour sponsored by the U. S. Government's Cultural Exchange Program. The protest to Congress was answered by Hy Faine, executive secretary of the American Guild of Musical Artists (AGMA), member of the panel which had selected the Graham company for the Cultural Exchange Program. He called Martha Graham "the greatest artist the United States has produced in the field of dance." This protest was registered while Graham's company was receiving its great acclaim in London, where *Circe*, based on the legend of the enchantress and Odysseus, was described as "a major theatre piece . . . a sumptuous spectacle . . . a symbolic fabric [woven] around Men and the erotic life."

40. "Fall-recovery" is the term basic to Humphrey's dance. It is a synthesis resulting from the interaction of opposites: periods of unbalance and relative balance. Humphrey explains that "fall-recovery" is actually three movements, the *fall*, the *recovery* from the period of unbalance, and the *suspension* held at the peak of recovery. She thought of the latter two as being one, and used the logic of weight, shifting of weight, and tempo in alternate succession of natural movements (walking, running) and in certain lengths and stresses for dynamic rhythms. While her idea for dance movement was basically that of equilibrium, she did not intend this statement to mean that the dance was purely a matter of keeping balance in the muscular and structural sense of the human body.

41. For a definition of ballet aplomb see Maynard, *The American Ballet*, Macrae Smith Co.

42. So keenly was Humphrey aware of "the drama of life" that when she was bedridden by arthritis and could hardly bear to hold a pencil she wrote: "To me, all dancing is a celebration of life." She personally claimed Nietzschean expression of philosophic thought as the interpretation of her own instinctive recognition of human emotion and meanings of movements. She quoted Nietzsche's two basic natures of man, the Apollonian and the Dionysian, forever opposed and yet coexistent in each man and every group of men. These she took, for her purposes in dance, as symbols for man's struggle for progress and his desire for stability; i.e., *fall-recovery*. Nietzsche propounded that this opposition and coexistence of the "Apollo" and "Dionysus" natures was the basis of

Greek tragedy, of all dramatic movement, and especially of dance.

43. Terms associated with Weidman's dance are "kinetic pantomime," "intensity" and "distorted opposition." These did not contradict Humphrey's principles but emphasized and accented plot and characterization in the Humphrey-Weidman works. It is generally accepted that Humphrey's theories were directed chiefly to choreography in large scale, and that Weidman's were almost entirely concerned with the stylization of pantomimic movement. Weidman's theories were new and set valuable precedents for the dance. But Weidman, like many of the great Modern dancers, eclipsed all his own pupils within his special forte. (Limón is by temperament and in style altogether more Humphrey's artistic product than Weidman's.) Weidman was very bold and frank in his creative work and in empathy with his roles.

44. Wigman, Holm's teacher, elaborated the subjective, emotional qualities of dynamic movement through physico-muscular means. Holm's theories were directed toward the analysis of movement. There are more than a dozen terms associated with her theory, many of them dealing with broken or axial movements as "curves," from which the "birdlike swoop" of the Holm dancer draws its designation. Her consciousness of space, actual and created, and of space as an emotional element in dance is part of the complex and immensely important analysis of the German Modern Dance. The American dancer whose original theories come closest to German dance is Graham. The Germans Laban and Wigman were strongly

conscious of pulsations in movement (*Anspannung und Abspannung*), the ebb and flow of muscular impulse. But this same consciousness was a principle of Duncan dance. She expressed it in poetic language as the rhythms of the human breath and the ocean waves: "And when we come to the movements of organic nature, it would seem that all free natural movements conform to the law of wave movement: the flight of birds, for instance . . . it is the alternate attraction and resistance of the law of gravity that causes this wave movement." (The student should note this poetic interpretation of Duncan's theory and compare it to Graham's and Humphrey's, to Wigman's and the German theorists'.) Duncan did not neglect "human experience" in her dance. She used it before the Germans. Margherita Duncan writes:

"Early in her career, she conceived a dance typifying human experience which was like a mirror of her own subsequent life. It was not born of any piece of music, but of her own thoughts. She danced it sometimes without music . . . her audiences loved it . . . and named it 'Death and the Maiden' after Schubert's song."

In Paris, audiences clamored for *La Jeune Fille et la Mort* for her program encore finale. These are some few of the many facts which place Isadora Duncan at the source of Modern Dance theories and principles for the German as well as the American twentieth-century dance. As early as 1909 Duncan stated: "All movement on earth is governed by the law of gravitation, by attraction and repulsion, resistance and yielding; it is that which makes up the rhythm of the dance." The national treatment of "space" which characterizes German and American Modern Dance was expressed by the critic Margaret Lloyd: "Duncan moved as a sculptural figure, as it were, self-contained and complete, regardless of physical surroundings . . . Wigman's attitude to the subject [of spatial problems] was emotional; she felt space as the medium through which she moved in much the same way as the swimmer feels water." Holm's developments in American Modern Dance are largely concerned with the incorporating and adapting of German principles of spatial relationships within the dance.

45. Two other important influences, in this era, came from the West Coast in Carmelita Maracci and Lester Horton. Maracci, equally the mistress of Spanish and ballet techniques, is also a Modern dancer. A solitary genius, she is not as well known to the audience en masse as to her colleagues. Lester Horton, who died in 1953 aged forty-seven, left his estimable reputation entrenched in the Lester Horton Dance Theatre, a repertory company which produced major talents. Merce Cunningham was a member of the company in 1938. Among Horton's best-known pupils is Carmen de Lavallade, an exquisite Negro dancer whose techniques range from opera ballet through Modern Dance to pure jazz. Horton worked in Los Angeles from 1928, independent of contemporary influences. It is notable that some of his compositions predate those of Graham and Humphrey in like theories and forms. Many contemporary dancers employ Horton techniques, ignorant of their source. Long neglected, Horton is only now coming into his justified renown as one of the chief innovators of Modern Dance. His techniques specialized in magnificent control, especially in lyrical movement.

46. Physical education, the buttress of Modern Dance in the

United States educational system, owes a great deal to Bird Larsen, an American of Scandinavian descent, for its inclusion into the college curriculum. Larsen was a physical education teacher at Barnard College, New York, who formed a system of "natural rhythmic expressions" out of her research in orthopedics. She later devoted herself to dance techniques; subsequently, her theories affected the entire system of physical educational dance. Her pupil Esther Junger was the first recipient of a dance fellowship from Bennington College (1937) and a major Modern dancer and choreographer.

47. Examples of abstract dance include James Waring's surrealistic dancing performed before a wall decorated with a skull, a telephone and a copy of *Time* magazine; Merce Cunningham's thesis that "anything can follow anything," that sequence and continuity are totally irrelevant; and Erick Hawkins's cryptic condensations of movement with startlingly imperative titles like "INSIDE WONDER OR WHALES" and "(effortless) now: like DARLING" from his *Here And Now With Watchers*. Abstract choreographers share to a great extent a reliance on unemotional or "heartless" music; music which does not literally lend itself to classification as tone poem, mood and feeling. But their methods, movement ideas and motives differ with such individuality that the apparently themeless body of abstract dance possesses electric personal significance from each major choreographer. As Balanchine's abstract ballet is wholly recognizable as itself so are the works of the abstract Modern dancers Cunningham, Hawkins, Taylor, Litz and others. But it must be understood that however free and experimental the abstract dance is in its choreography it is performed by con-

temporary dancers of extraordinary technical accomplishments. The contemporary dancer is not an unskilled
amateur but a professional of explicit training and technique, in the same class but in a different style from
the ballet artiste. Nor is the dance mere improvisation.
Cunningham has certain devices for "choreography by
chance," such as sketching on separate slips of paper
isolated actions of parts of the human body, of a hand, an
arm, a foot, a leg, a head, a torso, and then shuffling
these slips of paper and drawing from them "by chance"
choice the isolated "actions" from which to compose his
dance. Pauline Koner, the most virtuoso technician among
contemporary dancers, teaches that each limb must be
trained to its maximum potential for the body to lend itself to any style, and in order for the dancer to move in
every possible way. Katherine Litz treats each part of the
human body as an instrument in a whole orchestration of
movement and plays one "instrument" against the other in
subtleties of time and rhythm. Litz is chiefly interested in
exploration of movement qualities in juxtaposition, and
in spatial terms. Instead of a dilettante interest in dance,
the contemporary choreographers evince an intellectual
preoccupation with movement so unemotional that it
may have drawn their dance closer to science than to art.
Surrealism in Modern Dance has been influenced by, and
contributes to, the era's "theatre of the absurd," although
some brilliant creative dancers, of which Koner is the foremost, are adamant in expressing dance in human terms regardless of the phase.

48. To cite Balanchine's abstract ballet, this style of dance
does not seek an invention of new movement, as did
Modern Dance, but relates its abstract mode to the clas-

sical technique of the theatre dance. Its exploration is not in new movement but in new ideas for the ballet's gesture, tempo and rhythmic emphasis. As it has done before, the abstract ballet sometimes experiments with daring inversions of its form, turning "in" instead of "out" in deliberate negation of one of its principles. The neoclassical or twentieth-century ballet of abstract genre is qualified by an austerity or absence of feeling, and a preoccupation with geometric pattern and design. The hip and the knee, rather than the spine, form the fulcrum of the dance movement. As result, a typical Balanchine dancer has a certain technique, and Balanchine ballet is a distinctive choreographic innovation.

49. Some dancers have consciously related their work to that of painters. Merle Marsicano, whose approach to the dance of experience is spontaneous rather than analytical, claimed the influence of Jackson Pollock on her early work. Pollock (1912-1956) was an American painter whose techniques in abstract art are referred to as nonfigurative and "drip" painting.

Index